The Business of Selling

The
Business of Selling

How to Be Your Own Sales Manager

Anthony Alessandra, Ph.D.
Jim Cathcart

Business of Selling: How to Be Your Own Sales Mana

ISBN: 0-9625161-3-9

Library of Congress Catalog Card Number: 98-88989

Printed in the United States of America

0 9 8 7 6 5 4 3 2 1

Dedicated to

Our children—Justin, Jessica, and Jim.
We love you!

Contents

About the authors...

Tony Alessandra, PhD, CPAE, CSP author of the business best sellers Non-Manipulative Selling and The Art of Managing People, helps companies achieve market dominance through specific strategies designed to outmarket, outsell, and outservice the competition. Audiences learn how to get and keep profitable customers by applying Dr. Alessandra's high-tech and high-touch marketing, sales, service, and relationship-building skills.

Tony has a street-wise, college-smart perspective on business, having fought his way out of Hell's Kitchen in NYC to eventually realizing success as a graduate professor of marketing, business author, and co-founder of MentorU.com, an online e-learning company of world-class business experts providing training, coaching, and mentoring utilizing the latest Internet technologies.

Tony Alessandra reaches people — from the Board of Directors to the front-line folks in the trenches. He gets across information "with a lot of snap" — so people can grasp it, remember it, and use it. Recognized by Meetings & Conventions Magazine as "one of America's most electrifying speakers," he was inducted into the Speaker Hall of Fame in 1985—and is a member of the Speakers Roundtable, a group of 20 of the world's top professional speakers.

To reach Tony Alessandra • (800) 222-4383 • www.alessandra.com • tony@alessandra.com

Jim Cathcart, CPAE, CSP Professional Speaker and founder of Cathcart Institute, Inc. is the author of twelve books including two best sellers. His two-decade-long study of applied behavioral science has resulted in a breakthrough work in the field of self-awareness. In the year 2000, his book, The Acorn Principle was the #2 national best selling e-book out of over 2,000 titles.

As the author of The Eight Competencies of Relationship Selling, Mr. Cathcart has long been a trendsetter in the business community. His belief is that business should be practiced primarily as an act of friendship rather than primarily as a process of negotiation. This concept has come to dominate the business mindset since it was first published in his book Relationship Selling in the mid 1980s. Today he focuses on advancing the two elements that cause businesses to grow: Solutions and Connections. Among professional speakers Jim Cathcart is a world leader. Recipient of The Golden Gavel Award from Toastmasters International for 2001, Past President of the National Speakers Association (NSA), winner of the Cavett Award, member of the Speaker Hall of Fame (CPAE), Certified Speaking Professional (CSP), and a member of the exclusive Speakers Roundtable, 20 of the world's top speakers.

To reach Jim Cathcart • (858) 456-3813
www.cathcart.com • jim@cathcart.com

Preface

One very clear difference between excellent salespeople and those who merely survive is this:

Excellent salespeople think and act as the owners of their sales careers.

Mediocre salespeople think and act merely as representatives of their firms.

We believe that a successful salesperson must think more like the owner of a business. Successful salespeople invariably have grown past the "sales rep" stage into the top levels of professionalism. A professional is defined not by the business he is in, but rather by the way he is in business. A professional salesperson takes full responsibility for his or her business; develops long and short range plans which are consistent with the product, the company and the market; acquires, one by one, the skills needed for high-level success; and places *client satisfaction* as the top priority.

Sales managers the world over have told us that they want their people to be "self-starters." This book will enable salespeople to enter that elite group of self-starters and top performers who answer to the ultimate boss—themselves. They will learn strategies and tactics for managing their accounts, their territory and themselves.

The bottom-line result of using this book will be increased sales— but more important are increased self-confidence, more control over your career, and increased client satisfaction with you, your company, and your products/services.

In writing this book, we have drawn liberally from our previous articles, books and hundreds of sales seminars throughout the world presented to thousands of salespeople selling countless tangible and intangible products and services.

We would like to thank the people who have contributed to the development and refinement of this book and to those who have helped us grow as individuals. It is impractical to list all the mentors, teachers, role models and friends who have touched our lives. We would, however, like to acknowledge a select few for their special contributions.

Phillip S. Wexler, the co-author of Non Manipulative Selling, provided a tremendous amount of content and inspiration for this book. The ideas and examples he provided us through numerous phone calls and personal meetings cannot be calculated. We sincerely thank you Phil, for your sales expertise and your willingness to share it with us unselfishly.

Vital input was received either directly or through the works of Steve Curtis, Merrill Douglas, Del Dowdell, Harold Gash, Fred Herman, Alan Lakein, Dr. John Lee, John T. Molloy, Earl Nightingale, Joel Weldon, Peter Wheeler, and Joe D. Willard.

Our completion of the manuscript depended heavily on the contributions of Marsha Field, Karen Morse, and Terri Trotter. Without their help you might be hearing this material on cassette rather than reading it.

For their continued support and belief in us during the long writing process, we also acknowledge our 'sources of strength'—our wives, Sue Alessandra and Paula Cathcart.

Tony Alessandra, PhD, CPAE
Jim Cathcart, CPAE

one

Introduction: The Business Side of Selling

You can become a selling superstar simply by learning how to ride a bicycle. Not just any bicycle, mind you—the *sales* bicycle. And not just by riding it, but by mastering the art of maneuvering it. You must learn how to move the pedals to get maximum "drive" from the back wheel and to move the handlebars to get accurate "direction" from the front wheel. When you can do that, you will reach the "destination" of success both in earnings and prestige in your sales career. Want to know more about the sales bicycle and how you can master riding it? Read on.

The back wheel of our sales bicycle represents the business skills that give your sales career drive. It consists of the self-management and sales planning skills that help you call on the right people at the right time with the right product or service. The back wheel skills (business side) of selling are the primary focus of this book.

The front wheel of the sales bicycle represents the inter-personal selling skills that provide you with direction. Sales communications and face-to-face selling techniques are front wheel skills. More specifically, your sales communications expertise encompasses your verbal and nonverbal communications skills as well as your ability to "size up" prospects and be flexible in communicating with them. Your face-to-face (conversational) selling skills include your expertise in telephone techniques and correspondence, creating favorable impressions (image), studying prospect needs/problems (information gathering), proposing relevant solutions (presentation), confirming the sale (commitment and implementation), and assuring customer satisfaction (follow-through). They are covered in great detail in our other books.

Now back to the back wheel—the focus of this book. The "self-management" selling skills are discussed in three chapters. Chapter 2 covers the entire concept of professionalism in sales. Such topics as image, trust, attitude, sensitivity, empathy, maturity, honesty, humor, and enthusiasm are discussed in depth. "Your Sales Career and Your Life" is Chapter 3; it emphasizes the importance of goal setting in the salesperson's scheme of success. Balanced goal setting is stressed in the seven key areas of life—career, family, financial, mental, physical, social, and spiritual. Specific pointers are given on how to set and achieve goals and how to improve your self-image. Finally, Chapter 4 delves into the all-important topic of time management. Here we explore such topics as "efficient" versus "effective" use of time, time use analysis, identifying and eliminating timewasters, "to do" lists, and procrastination.

The section on "sales planning" skills is handled in four chapters which focus on territory management/sales planning, prospecting, promotional strategies, and call preparation. The chapter on territory management and sales planning is one of the cornerstones of this book. It provides explicit instructions on creating the sales plan through the S-O-S-C concept: Situation analysis, Objectives, Strategies, and Controls. Techniques and worksheets for completing a competition analysis, target market analysis, account analysis, and product/service analysis are presented. In addition, it covers recordkeeping, call frequency planning, and key account worksheets. The ideas and forms in this chapter alone could dramatically increase your sales effectiveness.

The sixth chapter covers the crucial subject of prospecting. Without a good flow of *qualified* prospects, even the best face-to-face salesperson would eventually fail. Sources of prospects, creative ways to reach them, qualifying them, and monitoring their progress from "prospect" to "client" are covered here.

Chapter 7 on promotional strategies explores various ways you can create "visibility" in your market area so that prospects will come to you when they're ready to buy. Advertising, sales promotion, public relations, and publicity strategies are examined as methods of creating positive visibility in your target markets.

The final chapter in the sales planning section handles call preparation. This includes developing market intelligence and setting call objectives for each account and sales call. A call planning guide is provided to help you determine important elements in advance for each sales call: information-gathering questions, unique features to present, potential objections and answers to them, and the commitment you will ask from the decision maker. This guide should take all the guesswork and "winging it" out of your future sales calls. However, it still allows you to be quite flexible on your sales calls because you're prepared for them. Remember that the best spontaneity comes from intense preparation. As professional speaker Joel Weldon says, "Preparation compensates for a lack of talent."

With the above concepts in place, our sales bicycle would look like Figure 1-1.

BACK WHEEL	FRONT WHEEL
DRIVE	DIRECTION
"Business of Selling"	"Interpersonal Selling"
SELF-MANAGEMENT	SALES COMMUNICATIONS
Professionalism	Verbal Communications
Goal Setting	Nonverbal Communications
Time Management	How to "Size-Up" People
SALES PLANNING/	(NON-MANIPULATIVE)
TARGET MARKETING	CONVERSATIONAL SELLING
Territory/Account Management	Meeting
Prospecting	Studying
Promotional Strategies	Proposing
Call Preparation	Confirming
	Assuring

*We would like to acknowledge Larry Wilson of the Wilson Learning Corporation as the person who popularized the bicycle/sales analogy.

The goal of this book is to show you how to build a clientele, not just make sales. We will focus on selling in such a way that your customers will want to do business with you again and again.

To accomplish this, we are going "against the current" so you can see things from a totally different perspective. On your part, this will involve expanding your viewpoint and changing your vocabulary in relation to selling. You will need to see selling for what it really is . . . a profession. One which rightfully belongs alongside the professions of law, medicine, consulting, and finance. One which requires more than just a "gift of gab," a firm handshake, and a perpetual smile. The sales profession requires you to become proficient in all of the activities and skills listed under the sales bicycle in Figure 1-1.

Before you start feeling overwhelmed, let us assure you that it is not as hard as it sounds; however, it does require effort. Perhaps a salesperson should take an oath just as a doctor or lawyer does. The oath would clarify the key requirements of the profession and serve as a constant reminder of the salesperson's responsibility. It would clearly state that this profession is not to be entered into casually nor taken lightly, because it is a *career*, not just a job.

THE SALESPERSON'S OATH

I choose to be a professional in the field of selling. I make this choice knowing that selling has many requirements.

Selling requires caring. In order to truly serve others and to help people own the right product or service to fill their needs, I must learn to identify their needs. I must be skilled in the twin arts of probing and listening, for one without the other is useless.

Selling requires planning and study. For my sales career to endure, it must be built upon a foundation of solid planning for long-term and short-term success. I must study my products and services until I know them thoroughly. I must know exactly how my customer can benefit most from the use of my products or services. I must study the selling skills that will allow me to help my customer own the right product for his needs.

Selling requires strength of character. There will be times when I am tempted to make an easy sale that does not benefit the customer. At these times I must have the strength of character to avoid the sale and act in my customer's best interests. I must be able at all times to say that I have advised the customer to do exactly what I would do if I were in his position.

Selling requires determination and persistence. Many on whom I call will not buy my products. I must believe unflinchingly in the law of cause and effect (every good act brings a reward, every bad act brings a consequence). If I make enough calls on qualified customers with a professional attitude, I will achieve my goals.

Selling is dependent on the free enterprise system and is an integral part of it. Selling is based on the premise that one person's knowledge, skills, and handiwork can benefit another. It is further based on the belief that one should be compensated for providing a service. Profit is the incentive that motivates improvement and increase. Profit, whether financial or otherwise, is a part of ownership and with ownership there is always responsibility.

Selling requires responsibility. I must recognize my responsibility to serve my client well, uphold the principles of this oath and my profession, improve my own knowledge and skills, and profit from my labors. When I earn it, it is my right, for I am a professional salesperson. In today's society, a *professional* is not measured by the business he is in, but by the way he is in business.

SELLING AS A LONG-TERM OCCUPATION

The American Dream has always been to start at the bottom and make it to the top. We have been "Horatio Alger-ized" into thinking that climbing the corporate ladder is the road to fulfillment and success. Recent experience has proven that this is not necessarily so. One need not start at the bottom nor make it to the top to be successful. Success in recent years has been redefined as the achievement of worthwhile goals and the realization of self-fulfillment in achieving them.

There is no "bottom" in the field of selling. A 40-year veteran and a one-week rookie are on the same level when they go in to see a customer. It is the level of professional skill that determines which one gets the sale.

Selling has no seniority system. Just because you have been around a long time does not mean you are more professional or successful than another. Some 20-year sales veterans are said to have one year's experience repeated 20 times, while others grow more with each passing month and reach higher levels of professionalism in a short time.

Is a Salesperson All You Will Ever Be?

In other occupations, when a person has mastered a certain job his desire to grow leads him up to the next level. Thus, it is natural to be constantly building toward acquiring the boss's job—and then the next one above that.

Selling has no such process. It requires a different growth orientation. Rather than everyone striving for the position of sales manager, they are striving to become better salespeople. Being paid according to sales gives unlimited income potential to the professional who is dedicated to becoming a better salesperson.

This book is dedicated to making you a better and better salesperson. It provides all the information and techniques you need to run your selling career as a business—a highly successful, profitable, and ethical one. Let's get on the sales bicycle and ride through the rest of this book together. We're sure you'll find this one of the most enjoyable—and profitable—trips you've ever taken.

two

Professionalism: It's Not What You Do. . . It's How You Do It

When you think of a professional salesperson, what words come to mind? What about the *personality* of a true professional? Think of a few adjectives.

Now shift your perspective. Be paranoid for a moment and assume that business associates are talking about you. What words would they use to describe you when you're at your best? What would they say about you when you have an "off" day?

One more question before you put your pen away. Ideally, what words would you like to have them use when speaking of you? Take your time and make a list as long as you wish.

When we have used this exercise in our seminars, participants responded with self-descriptive words such as these:

Thorough	Friendly	Competent
Professional	Prepared	Cool and Calm
Confident	Self-Assured	Sincere
Knowledgeable	Polite	Well-Groomed
Honest	Creative	Caring

Interestingly, their lists almost always match the list describing a professional salesperson. How do your lists compare? Don't be concerned about the words they might be using about you now. There are many ideas in the following pages to help you change these if necessary.

In answering the question, "What is a professional salesperson?" we can safely say a salesperson is one who lives the words on our list. Now the question is, how do you convey to others that you now possess or are developing those traits? Certainly you can't put them on your business card or tell your customers, "I am honest, professional, efficient, funny and humble." There must be a better way.

IMAGE

Many elements in our career and personal lives combine to create an overall impression or "image." This includes obvious things such as appearance and more subtle factors such as attitude, body language, and knowledge.

We are constantly changing our images or reinforcing old ones. Again, look over our list. Choose from the list those words you most want to have used about you. They will provide you with a start in creating the right professional image.

YOU NEVER GET A SECOND CHANCE

Upon meeting someone, we can't help but form a first impression. It's almost instinctive. We note them physically and also pick up subtle cues intuitively. We unconsciously gather information about them in order to answer the question, "What is this person like?"

You never get a second chance to overcome a bad first impression. Whether this is true or not, you'll probably agree that those first few moments can often make or break a sales call. Creating a favorable impression increases the possibility that your ideas or products will be accepted. An unfavorable impression, however, can thwart your efforts even to give things away!

First impressions are formed from several inputs. Physical appearance is the most immediate. Behavior, no matter how subtle, has an equally potent effect. Seemingly insignificant details such as voice inflection, posture, knowledge, flexibility, enthusiasm, and a sense of humor all contribute to the total image you project as a salesperson.

TRUST

The principle building block of any relationship is *trust*. This is developed to a large degree through consistency. We can only trust someone we know, and consistency is essential to this knowledge. The professional sales relationship between you and your client should be handled as you would any important relationship in your life. Your client needs a reliable, stable salesperson. The more consistent you are, the more your client will trust you.

Take, for example, a banker who drives to work in a purple dune buggy, wears bizarre clothes, and plays acid rock in his office. Would you trust him? (Remember, trust is independent of envy.) You probably wouldn't, but why? The reason is simple. We have expectations. Our expectations cover people, places, events, and ideas. Expectations are as much a part of life as eating and breathing.

One of the expectations we have of bank executives is that they are conservative, rational, and low-profile people. Our immediate reaction to this unconventional gentleman will be suspicion and distrust. This doesn't mean we'll never trust him, only that it will take longer and he'll have to work harder to gain our trust. In the meantime, we'll probably do business with a banker who falls in our range of "trustable."

Our expectations hinge on stereotypes and these change with time, place, ethnic group, age, occupation, and so on. If you lived in New York City you would expect your dentist to dress in a shirt, tie, and white coat. If he appeared one day in beach shorts and a Hawaiian shirt you would be shocked. On the other hand, if you lived in Hawaii and your dentist appeared in a tie and lab coat you'd be shocked. So everything is relative. The point is that in any given place the norms are predictable and, therefore, define people's expectations. Therein lies the key to effective image building—go along with the trusted norm!

IDEALISM VS. REALISM

During one of our seminars a participant said, "People have to accept me for what I am. I'm not going to change just to make the other guy happy." This person has every right to feel and act as he wishes. It is his prerogative to exist in a vacuum of idealism. He should not, however, expect to be terribly successful as a professional salesperson. There are compromises and adjustments to be made in any relationship, especially the salesperson-to-client relationship. If being unique and not compromising is more important than making a sale, fine. This is a reflection of the man's values. In Chapter 3 we'll talk about getting in touch with our values so that decisions (such as this) can be made.

We're not suggesting you change who you are. Realize, however, that your relationship with your client is like any other in which you risk acceptance or rejection. We're assuming, because you're in sales, that you want to be accepted and are willing to work for it (this includes compromise). Knowing which variables will increase or decrease the likelihood of a good relationship strengthens your knowledge of yourself and the sales profession. Armed with this knowledge and the willingness to improve yourself, your expectations of success will come to fruition.

WINNING TRAITS

Man is a social animal and sales is one of the most social professions there is. In sales, more than anything else, you are out to "win someone over." Winning someone over will result in a sale—the reason you're in this business. If "closing" is all you're interested in, perhaps you should close this book. If you're interested in being a successful professional salesperson, however, you'll want to do more than "close." You'll want to cultivate a reputation and an integrity which will go the distance. To do this, people must appreciate you as a person as well as a salesperson.

People choose a career because something about it appeals to their personality. People who dislike other people rarely last long or make money in sales. So naturally the sales field is full of gregarious people.

As friendly as most of us are, some of us still need to work on one or more traits that will help us be more professional. A smattering of those traits was listed at the beginning of the chapter. We will discuss key traits that will make your contact with a client more conducive to a long-term business relationship.

Your Attitude Is Showing

Ralph Waldo Emerson said, "People seem not to see that their opinion of the world is also a confession of character." Chances are that if you think this is a miserable world to live in, then you're miserable. This attitude will be reflected in everything you do. The same holds true of your attitude towards your clients. If you see them as schnooks whom you can manipulate, then you'll never be a truly *professional* salesperson. One way or another, they'll pick up on your attitude and will want to have nothing to do with you. Then try selling them!

A healthier attitude is to see your customer as a fellow businessperson with whom you probably have a lot in common. See your client as someone who is worthy of respect, if for no other reason than that he or she is a human being. Your clients are the people who will make it possible to be successful. Think of them as valves through which you must flow rather than as dams (obstacles) who will stop your progress. Only your positive attitude toward them as people will ensure the mutual trust which is so vital to doing business.

Flexibility

In our attempts to be people of conviction and belief we often go overboard and cling to our attitudes as if they were sacred truths. This practice, whether it is conscious or unconscious, creates a rigidity and a lack of tolerance which is socially maladaptive. *Flexibility* is the ability to adapt and is one of the keys to making and maintaining relationships. In dealing with your clients, you'll often find situations in which you disagree. This is not the time for you to show off your intellectual prowess. Competing with them will only intimidate them. Would rather win the argument or win the sale? If you chose the argument, you should be a college professor and not a salesperson, unless you're selling textbooks. Even then, you should develop the ability to listen, consider, and understand the other person's viewpoint. Then in addition to making the sale, you might also learn something. What a deal!

Sensitivity

The ability to feel forms the basis for all human emotions. We can all feel, but the extent to which we feel is determined by our sensitivity. Unfortunately, sensitivity is not taught in school along with the other basics of survival such as reading, writing, arithmetic (and home economics). Instead, we learn to feel from our parents and from society.

All of us are desensitized by the news media. As we watch the news on TV we turn off the feelings that would normally go out to people experiencing hardships. We do this to protect ourselves. You simply cannot drain yourself emotionally every night in front of the TV. Considering our upbringings and our desensitization as adults, it's no surprise that so many of us have a hard time knowing what we feel. Naturally, knowing what you feel is a prerequisite to feeling empathy or compassion for others.

Professional salespeople need to be sensitive. The give and take of a working relationship requires recognition of the other person's needs. An insensitive person simply cannot recognize that other people have needs. Sensitivity brings you out of yourself. Insensitivity makes you self-centered. It is impossible to remain self-centered and succeed in sales unless you're going to be your own best client.

Empathy

Empathy is another quality that causes a professional salesperson to excel. Empathy is the ability to understand and appreciate how another person feels by recognizing those feelings in yourself. Empathy is putting yourself in that person's shoes and experiencing sore feet along with her, but feeling the pain intellectually rather than emotionally. Sympathy, on the other hand, involves actually sharing the emotional experience as well. To clarify the difference, imagine two bums in the Bowery of New York's Lower East Side. One day the bums feel sympathy for each other because they're in the same boat. On the following day, one of the bums wins the Lottery and is now rich. He visits his friend in the Bowery and can't help but feel empathetic. The rich bum no longer feels poor but knows what it is like to have been that way.

When communicating with people who are important to you, strive for empathy. Open yourself up to what may be happening inside them. Be sensitive to what they are feeling as well as what they are saying. This means being attentive and developing good listening skills.

Maturity

Maturity is one of those nebulous qualities which everyone thinks they have, even the immature. It is all the positive character traits (mentioned in the beginning) in action. It involves wisdom, self-knowledge, and a certain calmness and security.

To quote Max Lerner, "The turning point in the process of growing up is when you discover the core of strength within you that survives all hurt."

Maturity is the recognition of, belief in, and action based upon your inherent worth as a person. Maturity strikes a balance between all of life's needs (more on this in Chapter 3). And yet there's more to it.

Mr. Albert E.N. Gray, when President of Prudential Life Insurance Company, in a speech entitled "The Common Denominator of Success" said that the common denominator of success is that "successful people form the habit of doing the things that failures don't like to do." This is a mark of maturity. A mature person will recognize the need to do things whether she likes it or not. This also requires being a generally well-organized person.

A major step in an individual's growth process is the total acceptance of the responsibility for his own actions. Until that occurs the person is living with two sets of standards, one for "me" and the other for "them." People who take responsibility for their actions will be willing to suffer the consequences as well as reap the rewards of those actions. Mature people can admit mistakes and remain unflustered. Immature people try to hide their mistakes or deny them. Immature people have extremely fragile egos. It takes only the slightest provocation to threaten their self-esteem and self-worth. Mature people are more "thick-skinned" in that they know their self-worth and don't have to be reminded of it constantly. People who are mature face their problems head on, find appropriate solutions, and learn by their mistakes. Immature people "never learn." A mature person knows how to handle disappointments and minor setbacks without becoming self-destructive or defeated. A mature person has the philosophical awareness to accept that there will be times when things just don't go right. That's okay, it won't last forever. During those times, maturity helps you muster the inner fortitude.

Here's an example you can relate to. Recall the last time you went into a restaurant with a client and received poor service. How did everyone react? Did you find that the mature people remained calm while the immature ones whined and complained, thereby making everyone else uncomfortable? A mature person certainly would not ignore the bad service but would think of more constructive ways of dealing with it.

If there could ever be a panacea for the ills of the world, maturity would have to be it. It's mind-boggling to think of how different things would be if *everyone* was mature. Maybe in the 21st century scientists will be able to synthesize maturity and make it a part of our genetic code.

Honesty and Ethics

Ethics, honesty, morals, proper conduct, and conscience are all part of the same fabric.

Honesty is the quality of being truthful, frank, and sincere. Ethics involves behaviors and can be thought of as honesty in action. Honesty leaves no doubt in other people's minds. Your word is "as good as gold." Honesty naturally leads to consistency. Living ethically is its own reward. Being ethical means answering to a higher law and not waiting for a response.

In our day-to-day lives, the border between honesty and dishonesty is a wide one. There are lots of gray areas open to interpretation.

In some situations the solutions are not cut and dried ethical choices. Ultimately your conscience will have to live with whatever action you take. An interesting chain of events links honesty, self-knowledge, and happiness. It can be depicted in two ways:

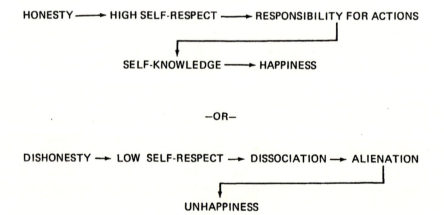

We'll use dishonesty to illustrate. When you are dishonest, you feel bad about it and your self-respect suffers (even if only temporarily). To reduce the discomfort that this creates, you do two things, both part of the same process. First, you dissociate the feeling from yourself. That is, you suppress the feeling. Making the feeling unconscious relieves you of the anguish. This is a highly functional defense during times of trauma. When used as a psychological "style," however, it becomes self-defeating. In addition to cutting off the feeling, you also disown the behavior. You unconsciously fool yourself into accepting the fact that the behavior was so unlike you that it's not worth being upset over. So the responsibility for it is avoided. This separation of your conscience from your thinking mind widens the gap between thinking and feeling. We've all experienced the widening of this gap at times when we've said, "I don't know *what* I feel!" When this becomes a lifestyle, the person is alienated from himself and from others to some degree. This precludes the development of self-knowledge—that process so essential to fulfillment.

This is all a way of telling you to be honest and ethical. You'll be respected for it and being respected is a big part of being a professional salesperson.

Depth of Knowledge

How much do you know about your industry? If someone were to say to you, "Tell me about this field you're working in," could you give them an interesting, in-depth explanation of how it started and where it is today? Perhaps you think that knowing the history or theory of your industry is not necessary for your day-to-day selling. It would, however, add to the depth of your knowledge and, therefore, your authority.

In all sales positions, the company has the obligation to educate you about the specific product you are selling. The company operations manuals will provide you with technical skills and product knowledge. This knowledge, however, rarely goes beyond that required to competently describe the product to a client. It is your responsibility to learn much more than elaborate descriptions.

Your independent research should start broad and end narrow, like a funnel. Let's say you're selling home computers, word processors, and the peripheral equipment that goes with them. The more you can learn about electronics in general the better off you'll be. You'll want to know as much as possible so that you can talk with your client intelligently.

Another reason for broadening your knowledge is so that you can continue to learn more and more in the future. A strong basic knowledge is the best foundation upon which to learn more advanced theories. This is especially true in electronics. The technology is changing so quickly that even the investors are confused. This is probably why many electronics sales positions are open predominantly to engineers.

After you've learned what you need to know to sell and as much background as you can absorb, you can then expand your knowledge of the specific product you're selling. You can go beyond saying "Daisy wheel printers are better than dot matrix printers;" you can explain *why!* As a consumer yourself, you're more likely to buy a product from the person you perceive to be an "expert." You'll have more respect for his words and products. There is also an implicit honesty when you can recommend something and back it up with an explanation.

The more you know about your industry and products the more you'll see how they fit into the overall scheme of things. In learning about computers you may begin to feel that you are helping people become more efficient, communicate better, and save money in general. This, in turn, helps their state of mind as well as the economy. So selling a home computer can be perceived as a more significant accomplishment than just "making a sale."

Talking about making sales—and we can't deny they're important—your specific product knowledge will help you immeasurably. Can you hope to make a sale if you have to answer every other question with "I'll have to check on that," or "Let me get back to you about that." Forget it! People don't want to learn along with you, they want you to teach them. If you don't have the answers, they won't have the money or the motivation to buy.

Keeping up with the latest developments in your field takes a certain amount of vigilance. If you let things go by too long, the amount of studying becomes overwhelming. For this reason, you should regularly set aside time to deepen your knowledge (and hopefully your enthusiasm and love) of your field.

Breadth of Knowledge or Idiot Savante?

The breadth of your knowledge determines the extent to which you can be conversant on a broad spectrum of subjects. Despite common belief, this is not necessarily related to a person's educational level. There are many Ph.D.'s walking around who know a great deal about only a handful of subjects—usually those around which their dissertation centered.

There are many problems with being a limited conversationalist or what we call an "idiot savante" (a learned idiot—someone who knows a lot about a limited subject area but very little about all the other subject areas). The most obvious problem is that it limits the number of people you can relate to and who can relate to you. To a salesperson this is a serious handicap. Another consequence of having a narrow fund of knowledge is your limited alternatives in intelligent conversation. Uninformed people tend to be extremely repetitious and boring. They also tend to talk about things that anyone can relate to, such as television. People can talk just so much about TV before the subject becomes tiresome and meaningless. A preoccupation with one topic, especially in conversation, merely shows how shallow the speaker is. Conversationally limited people often assume that everyone can relate to complaining. These people will start tangents about the government, inflation, pollution, communists, and anything else worth complaining about. They don't discuss them intelligently, they simply whine about all the injustices around us. Slipping into this complaining "mode" is a sure way to be labelled a "complainer." This is not conducive to establishing personal or business relationships. No one likes to be with a malcontent.

Anything worthwhile takes effort. Expanding your horizons is no exception. Since you are going to set aside some time each evening to bone up on developments in your field, why not spend some time rounding yourself out as a person. We're not suggesting you sit and read all night. By all means, get some exercise; otherwise, you'll certainly be a well-rounded person.

A fast, concise, and convenient way to know what's going on in the world is to subscribe to a weekly news magazine or two. These magazines will expose you to science, politics, the arts, international affairs, and so on. The articles are usually well researched and interesting, too.

A good newspaper scanned every day will keep you abreast of news and other goings-on in your area. Quite often businesspeople will discuss local issues more than national or international ones. You should be up on these. That doesn't mean you must have an opinion; being informed and "up to date" is enough. This will save you much embarrassment. People often ask you, "Did you read about so and so?" If you tell them, "No, uh, I was watching Captain Kangaroo," they're liable to look at you funny and move slowly away from you. And it's not your deodorant!

If you can find the time to read a book every so often, then you're going to be even more interesting. Reading good books, especially the classics, teaches why people have relished books for years. All of the suggestions we've given so far are, hopefully, already a part of your lifestyle. If not, you need to develop a little . . .

. . . Curiosity

"A man should live if only to satisfy his curiosity," says a Yiddish proverb. There is so much to know and do that it's a wonder we get any work done. The digressions are infinite; only our imagination is finite. And yet some people find themselves bored and lacking curiosity.

A healthy curiosity will provide you with the means to joyfully gather information. You will then become a valuable resource to both yourself and others. Your wealth of knowledge will simplify decision-making in both business and personal matters. Knowledge *is* the key to everything.

Stimulate your curiosity as you would your appetite, by nibbling on tidbits of information all the time. When you meet new people, engage them in conversation and see what you can learn from them. People are some of the most interesting "things" around. Not only will you pick up information but also leads and references to help your sales.

Force yourself to do new things. Go to the theater, visit museums, absorb the cultural and scientific life of your community. Do these things for yourself, not for your sales career. You have to take a genuine interest in your own development. The payoff in increased sales will come in due time. In the meantime, you'll be growing by leaps and bounds as an individual. People will recognize you as an aware and interesting person. This alone will increase your self-esteem tremendously.

Enthusiasm

We were so excited about writing this chapter that we couldn't wait to get started. Our enthusiasm was one of the driving forces that helped make this book possible. Your enthusiasm will make success as a professional salesperson possible, especially if you make it contagious. Enthusiasm shows your client that *you* are sold on the product. If he perceives you as an "expert", or at least as being credible, his curiosity will be piqued.

Your enthusiasm will tell your clients other things as well. From your enthusiasm, your good eye contact, and your overall sincerity they will conclude that you are an honest person. This will motivate them to establish or continue a business relationship with you. They'll become interested in you as a person in addition to you as a salesperson. This is what you want, both for yourself and your business.

Silent Messages

Body language is the popular term used to denote the "silent messages" your body gives people. When we talk to someone on the phone, we can only listen to the voice. In person, however, we can also "listen" to the person's body.

We all convey unconscious messages and give away our true feelings through posture, eye contact, arms, legs, and so on. The position and movement of our bodies tell the other person if we are

Nervous	Distracted	Open
Relaxed	Sincere	Defensive
Interested	Phoney	Affectionate
Bored	Receptive	Distant

It is important for you to be aware of your body language and that of your client. If, while you're talking to a client, he taps his foot and folds his arms across his chest, you'd better pick up the hint. Chances are he has better things to do or is too preoccupied to listen to you. This message would be reinforced if he was also looking around the room rather than at you. He's probably too distracted to concentrate. Picking up on his not-so-subtle clues will help you be sensitive to his needs. You can then acknowledge that he is too busy at the moment and arrange to come back another time.

Body language works both ways—you pick up your client's and he picks up yours. If you are aware of this, you can use it to your advantage (*not* "to manipulate"). One way of conveying sincerity and interest is to maintain good eye contact. You can also lean towards the person. This will "close the gap" between you. Proximity is another give-away. You've probably never read of or seen an intimate exchange between two people standing twenty feet apart. It's just not real. So if you're sincerely wishing your client the best of luck or sending regards to his wife and kids, you better not be shouting back into the store from your car. He won't believe you! The time to communicate genuinely is up close.

We recommend that you study body language and observe what people do with their bodies in different situations. (Try to be careful and conservative in your interpretations at first.) You'll notice that people are sometimes dishonest, but their bodies and voices rarely are.

Humor or "Did you hear the one about . . . ?"

"Conversation never sits easier than when we now and then discharge ourselves in a symphony of laughter; which may not improperly be called the chorus of conversation." Sir Richard Steele.

Humor acts as a social lubricant. It gives us something to share and helps create bonds of appreciation. We are automatically endeared to people who make us laugh. As a professional sales-person you would be wise to incorporate humor into your personal style. This humor should be the right kind, however, if it's going to be effective. Keep some of the following suggestions in mind.

Keep it in good taste. Know your audience and the type of material they will appreciate. Some people are more inhibited than others. Respect their standards of good taste—use discretion.

Be sensitive to your client's needs. Does this sound familiar? It applies to humor as well. If you're making them laugh, don't assume that your being "on a roll" justifies going on indefinitely. Be aware of your client's body language (because his verbal language will sound like laughter), and if it indicates that it's time to get back to work, then get back to work! People appreciate digressions as long as they are short and sweet. You don't want to be known as "that clown who doesn't know when to stop."

Original jokes are better than the old standards. If you rehash all the jokes that have been circulating for years, you'll be regarded as a jerk rather than a funny guy. Tell jokes that you know are new and unique. The best jokes are original, spontaneous lines which flow with the conversation or the ideas being discussed.

Look for humor in everyday life. This is the best way to improve your sense of humor. Some people believe that comedic ability is a God-given talent. There are others who believe you can cultivate it. Certainly you can increase your repertoire of humorous anecdotes and jokes. Most magazines and newspapers have a page of "laughing matter." Write down the good ones and practice telling them to people, especially your family. Another source of material is the local comedy nightclub, if there is one. Sit there with a pen and paper so you can jot down the gems. Most of the material you hear will not be copyrighted. You should always give credit where it is due. Never claim that a joke is original if it isn't.

The advantages of humor in sales are numerous. Clients will relax more readily with you. They'll appreciate and respect you. Most importantly, they'll remember you. So don't be so serious. Lighten up! As Romain Gary once wrote, "Humor is the affirmation of dignity, a declaration of man's superiority to all that befalls him."

Professionalism: Pride

Professionalism is a state of mind and conduct. It's not *what* you do—it's *how* you do it. There are many highly paid corporate incompetents as well as many very professional volunteers in every field. Taking pride in yourself and what you do is the seed from which professionalism grows.

Pride is the feeling of pleasure or satisfaction you feel in knowing that, as an individual, you are important, worthwhile, and (a) in control of your destiny, and (b) aware of and acting on your potential. It is this inner confidence which sets the professional salesperson ahead of the pack.

The professional salesperson will conduct business with finesse. She will carry herself in a way that is nothing less than admirable. She will have polish that reflects pride in herself and her life's choices. Pride will make her stand tall even when surrounded by giants. Professionalism recognizes potential and is therefore not stung by small disappointments or undermined by larger ones. Professionalism is "having it all together."

three

Your Sales Career and Your Life

For many years, people lived with the mistaken belief that their home life and their work could be totally separate. Many people gave their families and personal lives a back seat to their careers. For years they would chase only the carrot of success while other facets of their lives suffered.

In the 1960's the pendulum began to swing in the other direction. Young people in our country started questioning the traditional values of the "establishment." They denounced the work ethic and advocated recognizing people as individuals with needs which extended beyond work alone. They had a good point—but perhaps they pushed the pendulum too far. It is undeniable that a person's needs and identity encompass more than what he or she does for a living.

BALANCE

We all need to keep our lives in balance. It is important to realize and accept the fact that many needs must be fulfilled if we are to be well adjusted and happy. Our basic needs can be broken down into seven categories:

Mental	Physical	Family	Social
Spiritual	Career		Financial

In many ways we are like the fragile ecosystem of the environment in which we live. The different elements of our lives are interdependent. One need affects the others, especially when it is grossly neglected. For example, we all know that financial problems affect personal outlook, health, social life, and family life. It is for this reason that practitioners of holistic medicine examine all facets of a person's life when they search for the cause of a physical illness.

There is no escaping the fact that we are complex beings with complex needs. Our needs are dynamic rather than static—that is, they change. At one point in our lives the development of a career may require more time than our spiritual or family needs. At some other time, physical needs may be emphasized more than social or financial needs. Just because one need is more urgent than others does not mean that the others disappear. They, too, must receive at least a minimal amount of attention. Rarely can a need be completely neglected without unpleasant consequences.

To begin your sales career *effectively,* you need to work at bringing your life into balance. This requires *goal setting*—identifying the end results you would like to achieve for each facet of your life. Only then can you plan the concrete steps and intermediate goals which stand between your present situation and your ideal concept of yourself.

IF YOU DON'T KNOW WHERE YOU'RE GOING . . .

"Most people aim at nothing in life . . . and hit it with amazing accuracy" (Anonymous). It's a sad commentary about people, but it's true. It is the striving for and the attainment of goals which makes life meaningful. Lewis Carroll stated our point beautifully in *Alice In Wonderland:*

Alice: Mr. Cat, which of these paths shall I take?

Cheshire Cat: Well, my dear, where do you want to go?

Alice: I don't suppose it really matters.

Cheshire Cat: Then, my dear, any path will do!

No matter what kind of traveling you're doing—whether it's through your life or across the country by car—if you don't know where you're going, you'll never know if you've arrived there.

Taking "any" road will leave your fulfillment to chance. That's not good enough!

People who have no goals walk around feeling emotionally, socially, spiritually, physically, and professionally unbalanced. This can only cause anxiety. People who have goals are respected by their peers. They are taken seriously. It is a sign of strength when you make decisions affecting the direction of your life positively.

History demonstrates innumerable examples of the importance of goal setting. Can you imagine the following exchange taking place after Sir Edmund Hillary returned from Mount Everest:

Reporter: Congratulations, Sir Hillary! Tell me, why did you become the first man to conquer Mount Everest?

Sir Hillary: I was just wandering around trying to become inspired when I ended up on the top of this mountain.

Reporter: Really! Did it work?

Sir Hillary: Yes, but by the time I got back I forgot what my brilliant idea was!

You know this is absurd because a monumental feat such as climbing Mount Everest would take some serious goal setting and planning. Naturally, Sir Hillary had to work hard to gain the knowledge and physical skill necessary for the climb. He also had to acquire the help of a team of experts and procure all the equipment. The planning stages must have taken an enormous amount of time—longer, no doubt, than the climb itself.

The same principles apply to success in sales. You have to identify your goal and map out the steps that will take you there.

Goals Create Drive

Goals, when earnestly pursued, give people reasons to do some things and to avoid other things. We know a young man who has never been involved with drugs or in trouble with the law. We marvel at his good fortune and strength of character. When he was ten years old he set himself a goal—to be an astronaut—at last report he had graduated from the U.S. Air Force Academy with a degree in astronautical engineering. His goals were so important that he avoided doing anything to hurt his chances of success. Goals give us purpose and channel our energies.

Goals Affect Your Personality

It is easy to spot a person who has a clear set of goals. That person is the one who exudes a sense of purpose and determination. He or she has abundant energy and is willing to put more time and effort into any given task. Being goal oriented helps you become more positive, optimistic, and assertive.

We can think of ourselves as bodies of water. Someone with no goals is like a stagnant lake, spread out, with no movement. The lake just sits there motionless at the bottom of a mountain. A goal-oriented person is like a river forging its way through the mountains (obstacles). The river has movement. It is exciting and it carries things with it in its flow of enthusiasm.

In recent years many studies have focused on productivity. One repeatedly confirmed finding is that people who continuously set, pursue, and monitor their career goals are more productive than people who just "work at a job." Pride in and ownership of one's choices are important ingredients in career satisfaction and success. The uninspired worker goes home at the end of the day, having gained nothing more than a few dollars and a lot of aggravation.

Even on the factory-worker level, it has been shown that productivity will increase if a better incentive (goal) is provided for the worker. We all know that piece workers are more productive than salaried employees. This proves the WIIFM principle: What's In It For Me? The greater the rewards the higher the drive to attain goals. The individual chooses the goals with the most desirable payoff.

The Three-Percent Solution

Time magazine reported a national survey a few years ago which found that only three percent of those surveyed had *written* personal goals; 97 percent of the people had no goals at all or had only thought about them. They had not committed their goals to writing. Interestingly, the three percent who had written goals were found to have accomplished much more than any of the 97 percent. Almost every speaker, writer, and educator in the area of sales success agrees that committing your goals to paper is a necessary step in committing your life to attaining the goals. Later in this chapter we'll have you write out a detailed description of your goals. If you take the time to do this with us you'll stack the odds in your favor and be on your way to becoming one of the successful three percent.

The dividends reaped by investing in yourself are unlike any found in the financial world. When you clarify your values and set goals in all the major areas of your life, the right roads appear in front of you like mirages in the desert. Yet they are real! Choices become infinitely easier to make and you've taken a giant step towards living a balanced life.

BUILD YOUR FOUNDATION

Unfortunately, our society is very externally oriented. We judge books by their covers, people by their wealth or beauty, and jeans by their designers. Our culture teaches us superficial values by which to live and judge others. These values are not conducive to the development of inner strength, sensitivity, patience, thoughtfulness, compassion, or other virtues necessary for well adjusted, happy individuals. Yet to strive long and hard toward an important goal one should possess these inner qualities. This is true for any endeavor requiring inner fortitude.

I'm a case in point. I was once very much into playing the guitar. I played popular and folk music for years before deciding to play professionally. In order to play for money, however, I had to go back and learn basic music theory. I discovered that my foundation was too superficial to support the loftier structure I wished to erect.

The same principle applies to psychotherapy. Before a client can start on the path to being well-adjusted (balanced), his or her basic values must be explored and clarified.

Building a successful sales career is like building a house. If your foundation is strong, you can continue to rise on each completed accomplishment. If your foundation is weak, however, it could all crumble in a storm (such as a selling slump or weak economy).

SELF-FULFILLING PROPHECIES

When you stop operating under the assumption that things will go on forever as they are, you can then initiate some changes. More often than not, it is our assumptions that limit our perceived options. Negative assumptions set up internal obstacles which automatically defeat us.

One of the most common negative assumptions in sales is "I'll never get that account, why should I waste my time?" If you assume you won't get an account, then you won't! Either you'll pass it by or you'll predetermine the outcome by your attitude. Predetermining the outcome could be saying to the buyer, "You're not interested in this product, are you?" Ninety-nine times out of 100 she'll prove you right by saying "No."

Some negative assumptions in sales are

- "The economy is bad so people aren't buying."
- "I'll never make as much money as I want."
- "I'll never find a product/service I can honestly be enthusiastic about."
- "They don't need my product/service."
- "They won't like me."
- "I'm not smart enough."
- "They won't be able to afford my product/service."
- "I'll never call on *X* number of accounts per week."
- "A man will never buy from me." (for saleswomen)
- "A woman will never buy from me." (for salesmen)
- "People don't like salespersons."

This type of thinking usually becomes a self-fulfilling prophecy. You assume you can't do something and then you act in ways that guarantee your failure. You've then reinforced your original assumption. This could go on and on until you quit sales altogether.

Assumptions Dictate Behavior

Dr. Eden Ryl, in her film, "You Pack Your Own Chute," conceptualized the relationship between assumptions and behaviors a different way. She said: $A_1 \longrightarrow B_1$ where A stands for assumption, B stands for behavior and the arrow is read as "leads to." When you assume that you are capable of a certain behavior and *only* that behavior, then your actions will be consistent with and limited by that assumption. If you want new behaviors and higher achievements, it is doubtful that you'll ever achieve them until you expand your assumptions about what you can do. For example, let's say you want to set a goal of selling 60 units of a product or service within the next 60 days. B_2 is the new behavior you desire. A_2, however, doesn't exist yet because you've never sold 60 units in 60 days. So you need to expand your assumptions. Create an assumption (A_2) which says you *are* capable of selling that much. Then and only then can $A_2 \longrightarrow B_2$. You'll have allowed yourself to go beyond your old limitations.

Positive Thinking

In recent years there has been much criticism levied at positive thinking, probably because it has been exploited and over-commercialized. The fact remains, however, that positive thinking works. If you're serious about succeeding in your chosen field it will be necessary for you to cultivate positive thinking as a habit.

Self-Confidence

Self-confidence is the food which feeds our personal growth. It is an absolutely indispensable part of achievement. Self-confidence stems from the self-awareness of our intrinsic worth as individuals. We are blessed with an incredible amount of potential, most of which is untapped. George Santayana once wrote, "Man is as full of potentiality as he is of impotence." Santayana's thought also implies that the choice is ours, which *it is.*

Self-confidence works best when based on your own knowledge and self-respect, rather than on comparisons of yourself with others. A wise friend once said to me, "Don't compare yourself to other people because you'll feel either pompous or bitter . . . and neither one is desirable." So our self-confidence has to exist in a vacuum, and it can. It feeds on the knowledge gained from discovering one's inner potential.

Steppingstones to Greatness

After you've discovered your potential and taken responsibility for it, you can begin to become aware. Awareness starts with evaluating your strengths and weaknesses in the light of your current situation. You then expand your assumptions to accept more possible goals for yourself. This leads you to expand your actions and eventually to achieve your goals. The model for this process is:

AWARENESS ➞ BELIEFS ➞ GOALS ➞ PLANS ➞ ACTIONS ➞ ACHIEVEMENTS

One step leads sequentially to another. After an achievement you reevaluate yourself and find that each new feather in your cap makes you feel capable of accomplishing more and more. Your beliefs (assumptions) then expand, making more goals possible. The effect gains momentum and grows like a snowball rolling downhill. In this way, greatness is achieved through small "steppingstones."

The Filter

Ideally, all new ideas could start at the awareness stage and move on to the belief stage. However, something called a self-concept may get in the way. Our self-concept is the image we hold of ourselves. It is the evaluation we justly or unjustly make based on everything we have ever known about ourselves.

Most of us arrive at an inaccurate self-concept (we're negative thinkers by habit). This limited self-concept acts as a filter to limit the amount of new things we feel we're capable of doing. What happens is this: A new thought or feeling comes into our awareness. It comes up against the filter, which compares it to our self-concept. If the idea is consistent with our self-concept then the new idea is accepted and becomes a belief. If the idea is not consistent with our self-concept, however, it is rejected.

It is for this reason that the development of a healthy self-concept is one of the most valuable things you can do for yourself. Everything mentioned above, from eliminating "snups" to positive thinking, will help you improve your self-concept.

SELF EXPLORATION

In order to explore yourself and have a better idea of your values, we've designed a personal inventory for you to fill out. It consists of seven pages, one for each facet of your life: mental, physical, family, social, spiritual, career, and financial. In each of these seven categories we'd like you to write down how you see yourself. Your answers should be short phrases describing your strengths, your past accomplishments, and your current situation. (**Please note:** People have a tendency to read through a book without stopping to complete the exercise. If you want to derive maximum value from this book you need to read *and* participate in it. So please stop at this time and work this exercise. You'll find it extremely valuable. **Remember:** This book is yours. Feel free to write in it or jot notes in the margins.)

SELF-EXPLORATION: MENTAL

My strengths: _____

_____

_____

_____

_____

_____

My past accomplishments: _____

_____

_____

_____

_____

_____

My current situation: (Am I adapting/growing or standing still?)_____

_____

_____

_____

_____

_____

Things I'd like to change: _____

_____

_____

_____

_____

_____

SELF-EXPLORATION: PHYSICAL

My strengths: _____

_____

_____

_____

_____

_____

My past accomplishments: _____

_____

_____

_____

_____

_____

My current situation: (What kind of shape am I in?)_____

_____

_____

_____

_____

_____

Things I'd like to change: _____

_____

_____

_____

_____

_____

SELF-EXPLORATION: FAMILY

My strengths: _____

_____

_____

_____

_____

_____

My past accomplishments: _____

_____

_____

_____

_____

_____

My current situation: (Discordant? Harmonious?) _____

_____

_____

_____

_____

_____

Things I'd like to change: _____

_____

_____

_____

_____

SELF-EXPLORATION: SOCIAL

My strengths: _____

_____

_____

_____

_____

_____

My past accomplishments: _____

_____

_____

_____

_____

My current situation:
(Are my needs being met? Am I meeting the needs of my friends?) _____

_____

_____

_____

_____

Things I'd like to change: _____

_____

_____

_____

_____

SELF-EXPLORATION: SPIRITUAL

My strengths: _____

_____

_____

_____

_____

_____

My past accomplishments: _____

_____

_____

_____

_____

_____

My current situation: (Is my spiritual consciousness growing/deepening?) _____

_____

_____

_____

_____

_____

Things I'd like to change: _____

_____

_____

_____

_____

_____

SELF-EXPLORATION: CAREER

My strengths: _____

_____

_____

_____

_____

_____

My past accomplishments: _____

_____

_____

_____

_____

_____

My current situation: (How do I feel about my present job?) _____

_____

_____

_____

_____

_____

Things I'd like to change: _____

_____

_____

_____

_____

_____

SELF-EXPLORATION: FINANCIAL

My strengths: _____
_____
_____
_____
_____
_____
_____

My past accomplishments: _____
_____
_____
_____
_____
_____

My current situation: (Am I secure? Are my income and expenses balanced the way I
want them to be?)_____
_____
_____
_____
_____
_____

Things I'd like to change: _____
_____
_____
_____
_____
_____

Welcome back. Now look over the worksheets. What are the assumptions you've made about yourself? Are you justified in keeping some of them the same? What would you like to change? Make notes on those things you'd like to change. Again, be honest with yourself. This is only for you. This is not an exercise for anyone else to see.

BRAINSTORMING

Another valuable way of exploring your values and goals is through *brainstorming.* In brainstorming, you give free flight to your ideas on a specific problem to be solved. Opening your mind in this way can be valuable. By just letting ideas flow without judging them, you'll generate many times the ideas produced through the normal reasoning process. After the abundant ideas have been generated, you can go back to evaluate their usefulness.

Put these definitions at the top of each appropriate self-evaluation page—seven in all.

Mental: The functions of your mind—memory, concentration, learning, creativity, reasoning, mathematical ability, etc.

Physical: The many functions of your body—overall fitness, percent of body fat, skills and abilities, agility, endurance, etc.

Family: Your relationships with the special people you consider part of your family.

Social: Your relationships with others outside the family and outside your business.

Spiritual: The relationship between you and your Creator. Also defined as the philosophical and humanitarian areas of your life.

Career: Your involvement in your chosen field, both on and off the job.

Financial: The management of your financial resources and obligations.

Brainstorming unleashes all the creative capacities in our minds. It does this by removing the restrictions and guidelines under which we have been taught to operate. The ''rules'' for brainstorming are as follows:

1. *Suspend all judgment.* This is a time to remove your internal censor. Nothing is unimportant or too silly to include when brainstorming.

2. *Think quantity, not quality.* The more ideas generated, the better the chances of hitting upon something new and useful. Bad ideas can always be thrown out later.

3. *Extrapolate and cross-fertilize.* No matter how nonsensical it may seem, take your ideas to the *n*th degree. Combine ideas in unusual ways to stimulate new ideas.

4. *The wilder the better.* This is a time to be way out. Some of the best ideas are unconventional ones.

5. *Evaluate later.* Don't close your mind to any suggestions. Let the ideas percolate. An idea that seemed ridiculous yesterday may be ingenious tomorrow.

The Session

To brainstorm, find a time when you can be undistracted. Sit comfortably with a pencil and paper. The purpose of the brainstorming session should be stated in the form of a question or a problem to be dealt with. The question must be specific, such as "How can I increase my inventory of prospective buyers?" Once the question has been posed you should immediately begin jotting down ideas. It is important to record the first thing that comes to your mind. Don't judge, write! Make notes in brief phrases to save time. After the time limit you can fill in the details of your notes.

Brainstorming can be done alone or in groups. If you're working alone, a tape recorder is faster than taking notes. Again, speak only key words and phrases. Don't worry about explanations now. You'll know what you were talking about when you listen to the tape later.

After you have finished, review your notes. Examine all the possibilities as they come up. Discard unusable ideas only at the end. It is important and worth repeating that you should suspend all judgment during this exercise. Often wild and crazy ideas, when put together or altered slightly, turn out to be novel, effective solutions. So let yourself go. This is a time to have fun with a creative challenge. You'll find that you have a broader range of choices after brainstorming than you thought possible before.

Trial Run

Now that you see how the process works, we'd like you to do it. Pose a question to yourself. Write it at the top of a sheet of paper and then take three to five minutes to come up with as many ideas as possible. Be sure to put yourself on a time limit and aim for quantity, not quality. Take the time now to complete this exercise. Have fun with it!

Well, how did it go? Can you see how the ideas flow when you let down your defensive censor? Perhaps you even felt a little silly writing down some of the ideas. Would you feel self-conscious if someone read what you wrote? Fear not, we all have those feelings when we first try brainstorming.

Life Goals

Now we'd like you to apply brainstorming to your goals and values. The following exercise will stimulate your thinking about your goals for the seven facets of life mentioned earlier. Write on the following worksheets. Brainstorm each category using the rules we've just discussed. Allow approximately two minutes per page. Again, shoot for quantity and let your imagination take over. Begin now.

GOAL SETTING ACTION PLAN: MENTAL

What are my mental (intellectual) goals in life? _____

_____

_____

_____

_____

_____

_____

_____

What are my mental goals for the next three years? _____

_____

_____

_____

_____

_____

_____

What would my mental goals be if I had only six months to live? _____

_____

_____

_____

_____

_____

_____

GOAL-SETTING ACTION PLAN: PHYSICAL

What are my physical goals in life? _____

_____

_____

_____

_____

_____

_____

_____

What are my physical goals for the next three years? _____

_____

_____

_____

_____

_____

_____

_____

What would my physical goals be if I had only six months to live? _____

_____

_____

_____

_____

_____

_____

_____

GOAL-SETTING ACTION PLAN: FAMILY

What are my familial goals in life? _____

_____

_____

_____

_____

_____

_____

_____

What are my familial goals for the next three years? _____

_____

_____

_____

_____

_____

_____

_____

What would my familial goals be if I had only six months to live? _____

_____

_____

_____

_____

_____

_____

_____

GOAL-SETTING ACTION PLAN: SOCIAL

What are my social goals in life? _____

_____

_____

_____

_____

_____

_____

_____

What are my social goals for the next three years? _____

_____

_____

_____

_____

_____

_____

_____

What would my social goals be if I had only six months to live? _____

_____

_____

_____

_____

_____

_____

_____

GOAL-SETTING ACTION PLAN: SPIRITUAL

What are my spiritual goals in life? _____

_____

_____

_____

_____

_____

_____

_____

What are my spiritual goals for the next three years? _____

_____

_____

_____

_____

_____

_____

_____

What would my spiritual goals be if I had only six months to live? _____

_____

_____

_____

_____

_____

_____

_____

GOAL-SETTING ACTION PLAN: CAREER

What are my career goals in life? _____

_____

_____

_____

_____

_____

_____

_____

What are my career goals for the next three years? _____

_____

_____

_____

_____

_____

_____

_____

What would my career goals be if I had only six months to live? _____

_____

_____

_____

_____

_____

_____

_____

GOAL-SETTING ACTION PLAN: FINANCIAL

What are my financial goals in life? _____

_____

_____

_____

_____

_____

_____

_____

What are my financial goals for the next three years? _____

_____

_____

_____

_____

_____

_____

_____

What would my financial goals be if I had only six months to live? _____

_____

_____

_____

_____

_____

_____

_____

Once you've finished, feel free to go back and add anything you might have forgotten. When you're satisfied with your responses, look them over and circle the one idea on each page that stands out as being most important. Don't worry about what others might think or about what is socially acceptable. This exercise allows you to see your goals in black and white, on paper—where they should be.

Focusing In

You should now have a total of seven "semi-finalists" from the seven groups. Whether or not there is repetition is unimportant. Examine the seven goals, disregarding which group they came from, and choose the three that are most pressing to you. Write those three in the space provided below.

My Three Most Important Goals:

1. _____

2. _____

3. _____

Your Priorities

Now that you have separated those goals, look them over again. They represent the most important goals in your life at this time. Naturally your circumstances change from day to day and from year to year. Rarely will a goal endure for your entire life. Whether your goals are short-term or long-range, you can see that the exercise caused you to identify those things most important to you at this moment. You have become *aware* of everything available to your conscious mind regarding your goals. This alone is quite an accomplishment.

With all the insight you have at hand, it is now time to create a hierarchy of goals from the lists you just compiled. As valuable as it is to isolate your most precious goals, it is equally important to set out some less substantial goals for which to strive. So take the seven categories and list all the secondary goals which you feel are worthy of an action plan. You now have a better idea of where you are and where you'd like to be in every facet of your life. As an example, here is a list which I compiled for myself a few years ago:

- *Career Goals:* Make three more sales per week; earn a master's degree in marketing.
- *Family Goals:* Call Mom and Dad once a week; spend ten minutes daily with my spouse and each child.
- *Spiritual Goals:* Go to church once every two weeks; be more helpful to people every day.
- *Social Goals:* Go to monthly Rotary Club meetings; socialize with more salespeople and exchange ideas.
- *Mental Goals:* Stop worrying so much about money and success; improve my memory of names; increase my vocabulary proficiency; broaden my knowledge.
- *Physical Goals:* Eat less junk food; do stress reduction exercises every night; floss teeth every night; maintain an ideal weight.
- *Financial Goals:* Own my own home; purchase a sports car; provide for an ample retirement fund by the time I'm 55 years old.

Rules Of Goal Setting

Now that you've uncovered some goals, let's put them in a workable form. Certain rules need to be observed in order to make them effective. Goals must be:

Personal	Specific
Positive	Challenging
Written	Realistic

Most people, when asked, "What are your goals in life?", say something like, "To be happy, healthy, and have plenty of money." On the surface this may seem fine. As goals leading to actions, however, they just don't make it. They don't have the key ingredients necessary to make them *effective, workable* goals.

A goal must be personal.   This means your goals must be uttered with sincerity. It must be something you *want* to do rather than something you think you *should* do. Know your reasons for having the goal. Whether you want to achieve something for status, money, or good health is secondary as long as you want it badly enough to work hard for it. Remember W.I.I.F.M.

Your goal must be positive.   Try not to think of green elephants! You can't do it. It's an automatic response to think of the thing you're told *not* to think about. This is because the mind cannot *not* think of something when told to. We tend to focus on ideas and actions from a positive framework. When you think a negative thought such as, "I will not smoke today," your mind perceives it as "I will smoke today." You end up thinking more about smoking than if you phrased it differently. "I will breathe only clean air today" is a statement which serves the same purpose and is more effective.

Your goal must be written.   Writing a goal down causes effects which are a bit difficult to explain. It does, nonetheless, prove effective. Written goals take a jump in status from being nebulous thoughts (which you didn't care enough about to put in writing) to bona fide entities on paper. Perhaps their being written serves as a visual reminder and thus continually reconfirms their importance. Another possibility is that they gain credibility just from being written. We have been trained from childhood to give credibility to written statements. This can be seen in the statement from the movie, "The Ten Commandments": "So let it be written, so let it be done." When things are "put in writing" they become official in our minds. A written goal strengthens our commitment to accomplish it.

Your goal must be specific.   If you set your goal by saying "I will increase my sales next year," chances are you won't do it. You need to be specific to avoid the lack of commitment which comes with being vague. A more workable and motivating goal would be, "I will increase my sales next year by 10 to 15 percent. This revised statement has several advantages. It defines the increase which you are striving for as well as the range of the desired increase. Giving yourself some leeway is more realistic than expecting to hit your goal exactly on the mark. If you increase your sales 13 percent instead of 15 percent, you have still succeeded. You wouldn't have, however, if you had set your goal at exactly 15 percent.

Your goal must be a challenge. A goal must motivate you to work harder than you have in the past. It must move you forward. Set your goals just beyond your reach so that you'll have to stretch a bit. The more you stretch, the more limber your goal-achieving abilities will become.

Your goal must be realistic. Everything is relative to time and space. What is unrealistic today may be totally within reason five years from now. For years it was believed that the fastest a man could run a mile was in four minutes. It was unrealistic to aspire to running any faster until Dr. Roger Bannister broke the four-minute mile in 1954. Since then hundreds of runners have done the same. In any field, we never really know what the upper limits are. How, then, do we define realistic?

For our purposes, the best definition must come from you and your values. You must ask yourself, "What price am I willing to pay to accomplish this goal?" You should always weigh the payoffs and the sacrifices involved before coming to a conclusion. *Realistic* is ultimately your decision.

Goal Worksheets

Now that you know the rules for setting goals, you can apply them to the goals you set for yourself. On the following pages are seven worksheets, one for each facet of your life. These worksheets will be useful as guidelines for fine tuning and planning your goal-setting activities. It would be a good idea to make your own worksheets and use them for every primary and secondary goal you want to achieve.

Define your goal. Your first task is to determine whether your goal meets all the requirements of the rules listed above. If it does, then write it as clearly as possible at the top of the worksheet.

Examine obstacles that stand in your way. This is a time to guard against negative assumptions and other self-defeating thoughts. Remember the definition of realistic. An obstacle blocks you only if you let it. You should also write down your innovative ways of overcoming obstacles.

W.I.I.F.M.—What's in it for me? Why do you want to achieve the goal? What kind of payoff is motivating you?

Plan your action. You need to carefully list the steps you will take which will bring you closer to your goal. The smaller the increments the easier they will be to accomplish. There is a German proverb which says, "He who begins too much accomplishes little." As the American Dental Association is fond of saying, "Don't bite off more than you can chew."

Project a target date for your goal. State your deadline in a range, such as, "between March 15th and April 1st." Think carefully about the amount of time you need. Too little time will increase the pressure and frustrate you. Too much time may reduce your drive.

Know how you'll measure your success. Goals should be described in terms of the final outcome of an activity rather than as the activity. This is part of being specific. Instead of saying "I will be running more in four to six months," you could say "I'll be running three miles instead of two miles in four to six months." How will you measure this? Probably by having one-third more blisters on your feet.

When using these worksheets, feel free to alter them to suit your needs. The important thing is to fill them out completely and to *keep them visible!* Put them in a place where you will see them every day. Check off items as you complete them. Use them to chart your progress and take pride in your accomplishments.

Key Goal Action Plan
Mental

What is the goal I would like to achieve?

What are the potential obstacles that stand in my way?

Why do I want to achieve this? What's in it for me?

What is my action plan? How will I specifically achieve this goal?

What is my target date/deadline for achieving this goal?

How and when will I measure my success?

Key Goal Action Plan
Physical

What is the goal I would like to achieve?

What are the potential obstacles that stand in my way?

Why do I want to achieve this? What's in it for me?

What is my action plan? How will I specifically achieve this goal?

What is my target date/deadline for achieving this goal?

How and when will I measure my success?

Key Goal Action Plan
Family

What is the goal I would like to achieve?

What are the potential obstacles that stand in my way?

Why do I want to achieve this? What's in it for rne?

What is my action plan? How will I specifically achieve this goal?

What is my target date/deadline for achieving this goal?

How and when will I measure my success?

Key Goal Action Plan
Social

What is the goal I would like to achieve?

What are the potential obstacles that stand in my way?

Why do I want to achieve this? What's in it for me?

What is my action plan? How will I specifically achieve this goal?

What is my target date/deadline for achieving this goal?

How and when will I measure my success?

Key Goal Action Plan
Spiritual

What is the goal I would like to achieve?

What are the potential obstacles that stand in my way?

Why do I want to achieve this? What's in it for me?

What is my action plan? How will I specifically achieve this goal?

What is my target date/deadline for achieving this goal?

How and when will I measure my success?

Key Goal Action Plan
Career

What is the goal I would like to achieve?

What are the potential obstacles that stand in my way?

Why do I want to achieve this? What's in it for me?

What is my action plan? How will I specifically achieve this goal?

What is my target date/deadline for achieving this goal?

How and when will I measure my success?

Key Goal Action Plan
Financial

What is the goal I would like to achieve?

What are the potential obstacles that stand in my way?

Why do I want to achieve this? What's in it for me?

What is my action plan? How will I specifically achieve this goal?

What is my target date/deadline for achieving this goal?

How and when will I measure my success?

VISUALIZING: WHAT YOU SEE IS WHAT YOU GET

Visualization is an indispensable tool in helping people attain their goals. Musicians and athletes have proven that visualization is an effective substitute for real practice. In visualizing your goals, you will live your accomplishments in your mind's eye. The more of the five senses you can involve in this exercise the greater your chances are of accomplishment.

Let's say, for example, that you want to be the Salesperson of the Year in your company. You know that each year an awards banquet is given during which a plaque is presented to the year's sales leader. You may choose to focus on this banquet for your visualization exercise. Here's what you do:

Make yourself comfortable, close your eyes, and relax. Slowly and systematically go through all of the five senses. Imagine what you would be experiencing at the banquet.

Sight. Imagine what you would see there. You'd see other salespeople and their spouses. Imagine what they are wearing. You'd see tables decorated and waiters scurrying about. You'd see the bar and people standing around talking. Keep going for several minutes.

Sound. What would you hear? You'd hear the chatter of people. You would hear laughter, the tinkling of glasses, music from a band, people talking. You would also continually hear people coming up to congratulate you. Imagine that.

Smell. Imagine all the smells you'd experience. Women's perfume, food, alcohol, men's cologne, the smell of polyester suits (not yours, of course).

Feel. What would your tactile sensations be? You'd feel people rubbing up against you in the crowded room. You'd feel others shaking your hand.

Taste. Taste in your mind the champagne you'll be drinking. Taste the food you'll be eating. Experience the sweet taste of success! In advance!

Most importantly, imagine the exhilaration you'll feel when your name is called to receive the award! Take your time during this exercise and enjoy it. The more you can "visually" attend this banquet the more motivated you will become. (You might even learn something about the catering business!)

The Visualization File

To aid in your visualization exercise, you might want to start a visualization file. This is an envelope or file into which you put pictures, clippings, letters, and other reminders of what it will be like to succeed. Your file should also contain letters or awards which you have received in the past. Anything that makes you feel good about yourself can be included in the file. It can then be used as a source of motivation and inspiration, especially if you begin to feel a little down or demotivated. We all need to be reminded of our past accomplishments once in a while. Be your own best friend—remind yourself!

ROLE MODELS

Many people concentrate only on the goal they wish to attain. There's more to the picture. Successful people in every field have certain character traits in common. These common traits do not occur by chance, they are an integral part of goal attainment. It is worth your time to analyze the constructive characteristics of people who are now where you'd like to be.

One effective method is to choose role models. These are people to look up to and emulate. Your choices can include people who are dead or living as long as you are familiar with their personalities and accomplishments.

Harry Truman knew the value of role models. When he was in the White House he reportedly went into the Lincoln bedroom, looked at the late president's picture and asked "What would Lincoln have done if he were in my situation?" The answers to this question gave Truman the insight and direction he was seeking. It worked because Truman felt Lincoln was a man worth emulating.

In choosing a role model, several things must be kept in mind:

1. *Keep them off the pedestal.* There is no doubt that you will choose people whom you see as being "above" you because of what they have accomplished. That's good. What isn't good is to put them on a pedestal, thereby making them larger than life. We are all human. We all have strengths and weaknesses. You must not lose this perspec-

tive on people. Putting them on pedestals only further separates you from them.

2. *Isolate their strong points.* You need to look at the person you wish to emulate and analyze the precise qualities he or she possesses which you need to acquire. Sit down and write out the characteristics which seem to encourage their success. Use concrete examples of their behaviors which you can adapt to our own situation. For example, if you admire a corporate executive, one of the many traits you might isolate is her policy of "early to bed, early to rise." Write out approximately when she does each and why. You can then do the same and know the reason why you're doing it.

3. *Remain yourself.* Quite often the tendency when admiring someone is to try to become his or her clone. People who seem to "have it all together" have done all the "work" for you. All you have to do is imitate them. This is a dangerous way to think because you are not working on your own personality.

In the final analysis, you are you. It is impossible to become exactly like someone else. And why should you want to? So remain yourself while you acquire new traits to help you achieve your goals.

Sometimes it is helpful to have a symbol of another person's virtues. This symbol will actually remind you of that person and his or her qualities. It can take the form of a picture, a possession (e.g., your father's pocket watch), or some abstract thing such as a rock. It will be useful as long as it makes the association in your mind.

Multiple models. A workable system of role modeling is to examine the traits of several people whom you admire. This will help you avoid hero worshipping. Write down their virtues as you did before, without identifying to whom they belong. When you are with these people, look for more behaviors which reflect their success. The best models are successful people in your own field. Their behaviors are directly translatable to your life and will have more meaning to you.

Questions to ask.   Acquiring good habits from others will accelerate you towards your goal. Ask yourself these questions to get the most out of your role models:

1.   What would they do in my situation?
2.   What do they do every day to encourage growth and to move closer to a goal?
3.   How do they think in general? In specific situations?
4.   Do they have other facets of life in balance? What effect does that have on their well-being?
5.   How do their traits apply to me?
6.   Which traits are worth working on first? Later?

MENTORS

A mentor is someone you admire under whom you can study. Throughout history the mentor-protege relationship has proven quite fruitful. Socrates was one of the early mentors. Plato and Aristotle studied under him and later emerged as great philosophers in their own right. Mentors are worth cultivating if you can find one.

The same cautions hold true here as for any role model. It is better to adapt their philosophies to your life than to adopt them. Be suspicious of any mentor who seeks to make you dependent on him. It's better to have him teach you how to fish than to have him catch the fish for you. That way you'll never starve.

Under the right circumstances mentors make excellent role models. The one-to-one setting is highly conducive to learning as well as to friendship.

ROLE PLAYING

Role playing is like acting. You define a desirable behavior and then act it out for practice. Since "practice makes permanent," role playing will help you master new behaviors. It can be done alone or with a partner and need not take more than a few minutes. Like anything else, the more you do it the better you'll become.

Behaviors to Change

One form of role playing would be to get together with a friend and "play-act." Define a situation and the desired behaviors. Then run through it, trying your best to act as you would like to in real life. For example, let's say you want to learn to relax more as a salesperson. You and your friend would set up a situation in which you play the salesperson and your friend plays the buyer. You would then interact with the "buyer" in ways which allowed you to relax more than you have in the past. You would practice using more eye contact, holding your body in a relaxed posture, listening more, joking with the "buyer" and so on. Afterward, you and your friend would discuss how each of you felt during the exercise. You would repeat this over and over until you've made some progress. Role playing is an excellent way to introduce new behaviors in a relaxed, nonthreatening atmosphere.

Thoughts to Change

It seems that we are forever returning to the fact that we need to change our thinking. Perhaps this is so because our obsession with negative thinking is so great (and so great an impediment to our progress). Role playing through visualization is an effective way to change our thoughts. Basically, what you do is to imagine a situation and how you previously felt in it. You then think of more positive thoughts and feelings and practice using them in the problematic situation. For example, I knew someone who had a fear of asking women for dates. His typical thoughts in that situation were, "Why should I ask, she's going to reject me," or "If she rejects me, I will be devastated." He started role playing new thoughts in the old situation. Instead of his negative assumptions and extreme thinking he substituted, "I'm going to ask because I have as much chance of being accepted as rejected. I'm going to expect acceptance and will get it. I'm not going to invite rejection through my attitude. And if I do get rejected, big deal! It's not the worst thing in the world!" Through visualization he practiced and in real life became able to relax and approach more women for dates. (He's now happily living alone on a deserted island in the South Pacific.)

The Internal Actor

Role playing new behaviors can also be done through visualization. Instead of imagining what you would think and feel in a situation, you imagine what you would do. In your mind you can change the undesirable behaviors and have the new behaviors carry over into real life.

THE THOUGHT DIET

The *thought diet* is a tool that you can use on a daily basis to help you become the person who will achieve your goals. It breaks down those goals into daily actions that are bite-size and easy to do. By showing you the steps along the way, the thought diet will keep you from being overwhelmed by your lofty goals.

Rules of the Thought Diet

1. Read the thought diet card every day. It is best to read it *both* in the morning when you rise and in the evening when you retire. Repetition is an integral part of learning and will help you stay on target.
2. Avoid associating with people who drag you down emotionally. Associate with people who are positive and from whom your optimism can grow.
3. Make it meaningful. Read and fill out the card sincerely, don't just go through the motions. You'll be kidding no one but yourself.

Primary Goal

The second section of the card, after the rules, is a space where you write your primary goal. Write out as explicitly as possible that goal which is strongest and affects your motivation the most at this point in time.

Daily Growth

The third section of the card deals with traits you are developing. Write out five key traits that you need to develop to achieve your goal. State these personal qualities in ways which adhere to the rules of goal setting.

Action Plan

The fourth section of the card is the action section. Here you will write out the "minimum daily standards" which you will perform every day to move you closer to your goal. Again, be specific.

The following are some examples of minimum daily standards:

- Mental: I will spend 15 minutes every evening doing visualization exercises.
- Physical: I will do five push-ups and ten sit-ups every morning, at least.
- Career: I will read something related to my career for at least 15 minutes before going to bed.
- Financial: I will keep a complete record of every expense.
- Spiritual: Each day I will do one good deed to help someone less fortunate than I.
- Family: I will relax over dinner and enjoy a meaningful conversation with my family.
- Social: I will take time during my coffee breaks in the office to chat with co-workers.

Inspiration-Motivation

Read the thought diet card twice a day until everything becomes a habit. Once you've developed constructive habits you can move on to new behaviors. Fill out a new card and practice the new challenges every day until they become habits. In this way you will painlessly move closer and closer to your goals.

HAVING YOUR CAKE. . . AND EATING IT TOO!

There's more to life than making a sale, although we all know many salespeople who would argue that point. The fact is that having a balanced life will not only make you happier, it will make you a better salesperson. So have your cake and eat it, too!

Ultimately it all comes down to something Benjamin Disraeli once wrote: "The secret of success is constancy of purpose."

four

*Time Management**

Time is nature's greatest "force." Nothing can stop it, nothing can alter it. Unlike the wind, it cannot be felt. Unlike the sun, it cannot be seen. Yet, of all nature's forces, time has the most profound effect on us.

Time remains constant, but our *perception* of it changes. When we focus on it, it slows down. When we turn our backs on it, it speeds up. Our illusion makes us think it is something tangible. We arrange it, divide it up, give some to our friends. Sometimes we feel it is precious, at other times we waste it. We give it the power to heal when we say, "Time heals all wounds." It can also kill, as when we live stressful lives because we "never have enough time." On a day-to-day basis, nothing is defined and redefined in our minds as much as time. It's a wonder we can still recognize it!

Herein lies our power. Because things are as we perceive them, we can choose to see time as a manageable commodity and live our lives according to that assumption. It works, too! The first step is to take responsibility and *want* to control our time. This is one of the secrets of successful people—they work at shaping those things which others think are uncontrollable.

---

*Many of the ideas in this chapter were stimulated by the works of Dr. John W. Lee, Hour Power, Inc., Crawfordville, Florida and Merrill E. Douglass, Time Management Center, Grandville, Michigan.

As a professional salesperson, you'll have to manage your time effectively if you hope to be successful. Think of yourself as a business. Imagine having an employee who comes to work and doesn't get as much done as you'd like. It wouldn't be long before you started to manage his time for him. You would also watch him carefully to make sure he continued being productive. Certainly you can see that the employee is you. You are your greatest boss and your most valuable asset is time! This chapter will show you how to get the most out of this elusive resource we call *time*.

EFFICIENT VS. EFFECTIVE

In discussing time management, some people would argue that "What we need to be is more *efficient* with our time!" Other people would claim, "Let's not worry so much about efficiency, let's be more effective!" Of course there are always the ones who yawn and say, "It's just a matter of semantics, when do we eat?"

For the purpose of this book, we will draw a distinction between the two. *Efficiency* means doing things right. Effectiveness means doing the right things. Working efficiently is doing things with the least amount of wasted effort. Efficiency gets you from point A to point B via a straight line. Inefficiency goes in circles, zig-zags, and gets fewer mpg. Effectiveness means doing the things that yield results. Effectiveness takes aim at the target and hits it, even if it's behind you. Effectiveness *works*, often to the chagrin of efficiency.

The relationship between efficiency and effectiveness is

$$E + E = R \quad \text{where } R \text{ is results.}$$

It takes a certain amount of effectiveness and efficiency to obtain any result. As in math, however, the proportions aren't always equal. Using numbers instead of letters, the equation can be

$$4 + 6 = 10$$
$$3 + 7 = 10$$
$$5 + 5 = 10$$
$$9 + 1 = 10$$

In each case, the result is the same but the individual contributions are different. So too, the amounts of efficiency and effectiveness can vary for any given result.

Many new salespeople, when learning about time management, ask the question, "Which should I work on first, efficiency or effectiveness?" In theory and practice, the best answer is to improve your effectiveness first. Effective selling will get you sales and give you time to work on efficiency. It's much better to aim your sights at the result than to worry about the process. Too often we get bogged down in the means and lose sight of the end.

Like all the other changes to which we aspire, before you can improve your use of time, you need to know where you stand now. Taking the time to analyze your habits will lead the way to more effective time management in the future.

The first characteristic to learn about is your circadian rhythm. No, this is not a measure of your ability to dance to circadian music. Circadian rhythm simply marks the high and low points of your effectiveness during the day. Everyone has a "prime time." Some of us are morning people, others are night people. Whether this involves a biological determinant or not is secondary. What is important is to note your patterns of effectiveness. Find your best time of the day. Do you sell more in the mornings or the afternoons? Are you "in a fog" until noon? Once you know when you're at your best, you can organize your day to coincide with your "prime time." This is just the beginning of your gaining control of your most valuable asset—time.

The Time Log

In order to control your time, you have to know what you're doing with it now. We would like you to do an exercise which is going to take about half an hour a day for 15 days. You won't have to go on a crash diet or run three miles a day, but we guarantee that by the end of the second week you'll have grown. You'll *look* the same, but you'll have *grown* (inside, of course). The insight you gain from keeping track of your activities is what you base your time management goals on. How will you know which bad habits to change unless you monitor your present way of doing things? It would be like going to a doctor and telling him you think you need to lower your blood pressure. Would you be happy if he prescribed a drug without taking your blood pressure first? If you want to increase your sales through more efficient time management, you need to pinpoint exactly how. Otherwise you'll be as uncommitted as if all your goals were unwritten!

So take the time every day to complete the time logs. Fill in your activities for 10-minute intervals throughout the day. Try not to allow more than an hour to pass without recording what you've done. It's really not as much work as it seems. It'll be a habit in no time.

At the end of each day, you should also answer the daily time analysis questions. Try to be as exact as possible in ascertaining what happened that day. Also be specific in stating the ways you'll make tomorrow better.

At the end of 10 days, analyze the time logs to determine the six most important activities that you engaged in during that time. List them here in the space provided. At the same time, determine the six least important things you did and compute the total amount of time spent on each of these activities.

After you've written out your six most and least productive activities and the time spent on each, you will be equipped to set some time management objectives. Use the skills you learned in the chapter on goal setting. Write out your objectives and develop an action plan for each. Then, follow through! It'll lower your handicap.

TIME LOG FOR_____ DATE_____ DAY_____

| | | | DESCRIPTION OF ACTIVITIES | ANALYSIS |
HOUR	TIME FRAME	ACTUAL TIME		COMMENTS FOR BETTER TIME USE
7	0-30			
	30-60			
8	0-30			
	30-60			
9	0-30			
	30-60			
10	0-30			
	30-60			

TIME LOG FOR _____ DATE _____ DAY _____

HOUR	TIME FRAME	ACTUAL TIME	DESCRIPTION OF ACTIVITIES	ANALYSIS COMMENTS FOR BETTER TIME USE
11	0-30			
	30-60			
12	0-30			
	30-60			
1	0-30			
	30-60			
2	0-30			
	30-60			

TIME LOG FOR _____ DATE _____ DAY _____

HOUR	TIME FRAME	ACTUAL TIME	DESCRIPTION OF ACTIVITIES	ANALYSIS — COMMENTS FOR BETTER TIME USE
3	0-30			
	30-60			
4	0-30			
	30-60			
5	0-30			
	30-60			
6	0-30			
	30-60			

TIME LOG FOR _____		DATE _____ DAY _____	ANALYSIS
HOUR	TIME FRAME	ACTUAL TIME	DESCRIPTION OF ACTIVITIES	COMMENTS FOR BETTER TIME USE
7	0-30			
	30-60			
8	0-30			
	30-60			
9	0-30			
	30-60			
10	0-30			
	30-60			

DAILY TIME ANALYSIS QUESTIONS

1. What went right today? Why?

2. What went wrong today? Why?

3. What time did I start on my top priority task? Why? Could I have started earlier?

4. What patterns do I see in my time logs?

5. What part of the day was most productive? Least productive?

6. What were my three biggest timewasters today?

7. What activities need more time? Which need less time?

8. Beginning tomorrow, what will I do to make better use of my time?

TIME LOG ANALYSIS

MY SIX MOST PRODUCTIVE ACTIVITIES   Between (Dates) _____

1.   Total Time: _____

2.   Total Time: _____

3.   Total Time: _____

4.   Total Time: _____

5.   Total Time: _____

6.   Total Time: _____

MY SIX LEAST PRODUCTIVE ACTIVITIES   Between (Dates)

1.   Total Time: _____

2.   Total Time: _____

3.   Total Time: _____

4.   Total Time: _____

5.   Total Time: _____

6.   Total Time: _____

Eliminating Time Wasters

There isn't anyone who doesn't waste time, and anyone who tells you they don't is wasting *your* time! Of course, we really can't tell you what is a waste of *your* time. What constitutes a "waste of time" is strictly an individual judgment. One man's waste is another man's fodder.

A systematic evaluation of time wasters reveals that they come from the people around you as well as from within yourself. Some time wasters are unavoidable, but reducible nonetheless. You need to identify the most frequent sources of time wasters in your day. Use the worksheet, *Time Wasters*, to develop a profile of your time-wasting activities. Be honest with yourself and base your answers on an average day. After you've completed part one, choose the three biggest time wasters and enter them in the spaces in part two. Then think of ways in which you will overcome the time wasters.

As a means of comparison, we've included a list of time wasters compiled by Leo Moore of MIT. Most researchers find the same handful at the top of their lists, which indicates that they are problems common to all of us:

Telephone	Procrastination
Meetings	"Fire fighting"
Reports	Special requests
Visitors	Delays
Delegation	Reading

In all positions and occupations, there are time wasters—that is, areas in which we tend to lose or waste time during our work day. How much of your time is spent in these areas?

Time Wasters

	None	Some	A Lot
1. Overpreparing for calls.	____	____	____
2. Scheduling less important work before more important work.	____	____	____
3. Starting a job before thinking it through.	____	____	____
4. Leaving jobs before they are completed.	____	____	____
5. Doing things that can be delegated to another person (across or down; not upward).	____	____	____
6. Doing things that can be delegated to modern equipment (providing such exists in your work).	____	____	____
7. Doing things that actually aren't a part of your real job.	____	____	____
8. Keeping too many, too complicated, or overlapping records.	____	____	____
9. Pursuing prospects you probably can't sell.	____	____	____
10. Paying too much attention to low-yield prospects.	____	____	____
11. Handling too wide a variety of duties.	____	____	____
12. Failing to build barriers against interruptions.	____	____	____
13. Allowing conferences and discussions to wander.	____	____	____
14. Conducting unnecessary meetings, visits, and/or phone calls.	____	____	____
15. Chasing trivial data after the main facts are in.	____	____	____
16. Socializing at great length between tasks.	____	____	____

OVERCOMING TIME WASTERS

1. Timewaster _____

    Strategies for minimizing

2. Time waster _____

    Strategies for minimizing

3. Time waster _____

    Strategies for minimizing

SETTING PRIORITIES

When setting your priorities, there are two famous laws to remember. The first is *Parkinson's Law*. It states that work tends to expand to fill the time allotted for its completion. Parkinson's Law makes setting priorities twice as important. If you don't know what your priorities are, your other work will expand to fill in the extra time. It will take longer for you accomplish less.

The second law of note is *Pareto's Principle*. Pareto's Principle, in this situation, states that 80 percent of your results come from 20 percent of your efforts. Another way to look at it is that 80 percent of your business comes from 20 percent of your clients. It's also called the 80-20 rule.

Thus, if your time is worth *x* amount per hour to you, you need to spend your time doing things that pay you more than your time is worth. What is your time worth? To get an idea, look at the chart on the following page. With your time being worth this much, you need to increase the use of your time in high priority activities which bring the greatest payoff. It doesn't make sense to wash your car during the day when your time is worth $25.00 per hour or more to you. Arrange your day to take advantage of your earning potential.

Identify your high priority activities and fill out the worksheet on the next page. Think about the most important things you do from three different perspectives: your sales manager's, your clients', and your own. After thinking about these, choose the six priorities that stand out regardless of perspective.

**What Your Time Is Worth
Based On Yearly Income***

Yearly Income*	*Every Hour Is Worth* (40 Hr. Week)	*1 hr/wk of Selling Time Is Worth**
$ 5,000	$ 2.56	$ 128.00
$ 7,500	$ 3.84	$ 192.00
$ 10,000	$ 5.12	$ 256.00
$ 20,000	$ 10.25	$ 512.50
$ 30,000	$ 15.37	$ 768.50
$ 40,000	$ 20.50	$1,025.00
$ 50,000	$ 25.62	$1,281.00
$ 60,000	$ 30.74	$1,537.00
$ 70,000	$ 35.86	$1,793.00
$ 80,000	$ 40.94	$2,047.00
$ 90,000	$ 46.10	$2,305.00
$100,000	$ 51.23	$2,561.00

*Based on approximately 50 working weeks per year.

Using A "To Do" List

A list of "things to do" for each day and week is a valuable aid to managing your time. A "to do" list organizes your thinking and planning onto one form in the least amount of time with the maximum amount of efficiency. Such a list is especially helpful if it coincides with the record keeping you already do for your company. After a short time you will find yourself handling a greater

HIGH PRIORITY ACTIVITIES

DIRECTIONS: List below the six most important payoff activities you perform on the job in the eyes of your immediate manager, your clients/customers, and yourself. Then, come up with the overall top six activities regardless of individual perspective.

In the eyes of my sales manager:

1. _____
2. _____
3. _____
4. _____
5. _____
6. _____

In the eyes of my customers and prospects:

1. _____
2. _____
3. _____
4. _____
5. _____
6. _____

In my own eyes:

1. _____
2. _____
3. _____
4. _____
5. _____
6. _____

THE OVERALL HIGH PRIORITY ACTIVITIES:

1. _____
2. _____
3. _____
4. _____
5. _____
6. _____

volume of work without increasing your stress. You'll simply become more efficient.

Because we are creatures of habit, it's a good idea for you to fill out your "to do" list at the same time every day. This way you'll be committed to a routine and will avoid procrastination. Whether you fill it out in the evening or first thing in the morning is unimportant. You should keep in mind, however, that you are often in a hurry in the morning and may be tempted to skip it.

As we mentioned before, Parkinson's Law states that work expands to fill the time alloted for it. Your "to do" list should, therefore, define a specific amount of time (if possible) for each activity. This will keep work from "expanding."

Your activities should be listed in order of priority. Work on high priorities first and keep in mind what your time is worth. In listing the activities, it is helpful to spell out the result as well as the process. For example, you might list, "Between 12:00 and 1:00 p.m., go to manufacturer's rep luncheon and get at least three business cards from prospects." Stating when, where, and what you're going to do increases your chances of doing it successfully.

As the day goes by, check off completed activities and make any notes that seem relevant. In the evening, make out a new "to do" list for the next day and include any activities you couldn't complete the day before. Always save your "to do" lists for future reference.

Keeping Records of Time Use

Some companies require their salespeople to keep accurate records, others do not. The experts in time management all agree that the more records you keep, the more you will be aware of the opportunities for sales, for prospecting, and for improving your use of time. Examples of valuable records to keep include the following:

- Number of sales calls.
- Number of calls resulting in interviews.
- Number of interviews resulting in attempts to confirm the sale.

To Do List

Item	Priority	Time Needed	Done ✔

Notes

Scheduled Events

8:00	
8:15	
8:30	
8:45	
9:00	
9:15	
9:30	
9:45	
10:00	
10:15	
10:30	
10:45	
11:00	
11:15	
11:30	
11:45	
12:00	
12:15	
12:30	
12:45	
1:00	
1:15	
1:30	
1:45	
2:00	
2:15	
2:30	
2:45	
3:00	
3:15	
3:30	
3:45	
4:00	
4:15	
4:30	
4:45	
5:00	
5:15	
5:30	
5:45	
6:00	
Evening	

Reprinted with permission from Merrill E. Douglass, Time Management Center, Grandville, Michigan.

- Number of actual sales.
- Number of sales that stay on the books.

Through systematic record keeping you will learn, among other things, what phase of the sale you're having trouble with. You can actually graph or chart your performance to get a graphic illustration of your strengths and weaknesses.

Another highly valuable record to keep is your daily time log. Not only will this depict your efficiency on a day-to-day basis, it will also speed your writing of monthly reports. In fact, you might be able to staple your daily time logs together to compose your monthly report. If you get in the habit of taking five minutes each day to answer the time analysis questions, you will quickly gain invaluable insight into your patterns of both productive activity and time wasting. Like written goals, daily written proof of your inefficiency will have more of an effect on your motivation than just thinking about it.

PROCRASTINATION

"Don't put off for tomorrow what you can do today" (My Mother—ever since I can remember).

Procrastination is like a virus. It creeps up on you slowly, drains you of energy, and is difficult to get rid of if your resistance is low. Procrastination is a close relative of incompetence and a first cousin to inefficiency, which is why their marriage is taboo. We all procrastinate from time to time. What's important is not to do it on things that count. You can overcome procrastination, if you recognize it and take responsibility for it. Don't make yourself the "victim" by claiming to be "lazy." Laziness means simply not caring enough to act. These suggestions will help you conquer the virus:

1. *Choose one area* in which procrastination plagues you and conquer it. Set up a procrastination priority and action steps. For example, if you're putting off calling qualified prospects, simply set a goal of calling on X number every day or week.

2. *Give yourself deadlines.* In moderation, pressure motivates. Extreme pressure debilitates. Set appointments,

make commitments, write out your goals, and otherwise develop the determination to succeed.

3. *Don't duck the difficult problems.* Every day we are faced with both difficult and easy tasks. Tackle the difficult ones first so that you can look forward to the easy ones. If you work on the easy ones first, you might expand the time that they take in order to avoid the difficult ones waiting for you.

Many people put off difficult or large tasks because they appear too huge to tackle in a reasonable time frame. They feel that if they start and complete the "large" task at one sitting, it will prevent them from accomplishing any of the other tasks they have to do on that day. The answer to this problem is to break all large or difficult tasks into their smaller subparts. Then, you can do each of the subparts of the larger project over a series of days, if appropriate.

Several years ago, when I was writing my book, *Non-Manipulative Selling*, I procrastinated writing it (even *starting* to write it) past two deadlines from my publisher. Finally, the publisher informed me that my third and *final* deadline would be 90 days from that day. If I didn't meet this deadline they would ask me to return the advance money they had given me when we signed the book contract (Indian givers!).

As I entered my final deadline state of depression, a close friend gave me a very simple idea that helped me finish the book. He said that if I wrote only three pages of the book per day—the *very first* thing each morning—that the book would be done well before the deadline. Three pages per day seemed like such an easy task (and it was) that I finished the 180-page book in less than 30 days (some days I wrote many more than three pages).

The moral of the story is not to let huge, difficult tasks paralyze you into no action at all. Break them into bite-sized pieces so they're easier to chew and digest (as you can tell, I'm writing this before lunch).

4. *Don't let perfectionism paralyze you.* This is a problem which many writers have. They sit at their typewriters waiting for the "right" words to come out. What they are

doing is avoiding the process of writing. Be prolific in your activities. You can always go back later and polish those things you're unhappy with. Better yet, you can delegate the polishing to someone else.

Because humans are so susceptible to procrastination, you must work at building up your immunity to it. Effective action is the best medicine.

HANDLING PAPERWORK

The first step in handling paperwork is to do yourself the favor of reducing it. Delegate as much as you can to your secretary or other co-worker. After you've reduced the quantity, you can then handle the rest efficiently.

Have your secretary screen your mail. Have it put in order of priority so that you can act on the most important pieces first. Junk mail would be on the bottom. Important mail and information would go in the middle and letters requiring an immediate response would go on top. Set a time for opening your mail and keep it the same every day. This, obviously, should be scheduled during an otherwise nonproductive time.

Try to answer any correspondence immediately. After you've read the letter, write your reply on the back and give it to your secretary to type. An even more efficient method is to use a dictation machine or tape recorder. Record your correspondence and leave the rest to your secretary.

Some companies prefer to use form letters instead of replying personally. This is acceptable in some circumstances, but not when you're communicating with prospects or clients.

The other mail you receive should be dealt with in the same way. Act immediately on whatever you can. If you receive a magazine, peruse it and clip out articles you intend to read. Try categorizing your reading material into three groups: articles you must read soon, articles you should read, and articles that would be nice to read. Clipping the article makes it more accessible. Stacking ten articles in one category is much more practical than stacking ten magazines. The magazines look like more work and discourage you from diving into them.

Naturally there will be more than mail accumulating on your desk. Adopt a policy of picking up paperwork only once. This means you should not look at something and put it back down where you found it. It's much wiser to take some form of action on the item. Decide what to do with it and move it along to the next step toward completion.

One novel approach to correspondence was adopted by entrepreneur Meshulan Riklis. He simply let all but the most urgent mail "ripen" in his "in" box for at least three months. When it was ripe, he found that 80 percent of it didn't need to be answered.

YOUR USE OF DOWN TIME

Down time normally refers to time when a machine is out of service. Your down time includes unstructured minutes and hours during the day when you can't get anything significant accomplished. These periods arise during traffic jams, in waiting rooms, when people fail to show up for appointments, and so on. You can fill this time instead of "wasting" it.

There are ways of doing nothing creatively. You can sit and relax, meditate, or levitate. You can look at your "to do" list and change it if necessary. You can think about your goals or the obstacles that you face and how you're going to overcome them. This is a good time to do your visualization exercises. Imagine yourself calling on that account that you've been dreading. Imagine yourself as successful and you should improve your chances of becoming successful.

Remember those articles you clipped and saved? If you carry them with you they can be read while you're waiting for someone. It's amazing how many little tasks can be done in ten-minute time slots. Down time is also useful for making phone calls, unless, of course, you're in traffic. You can call ahead to your next appointment, call the office, and so on. With this in mind, you might want to write phone numbers on your "to do" list so they'll be readily accessible.

The important thing about down time is to avoid wasting it. Don't fight yourself and the world and become aggravated. Relax and see it for what it is: more of that valuable asset which you so desperately need—time.

INTERRUPTIONS

Most people who phone or visit you at home or work do so under a false yet unquestioned assumption that you are free and "receiving" company. No one ever calls and says, "Hi, are you busy?" Or if they do it's, "Hi, are you busy?" (Yes) . . . "Oh, good . . . I wanted to tell you about this delicious pastrami sandwich I just had . . . " Just what you need to hear in the middle of a busy day! It's no wonder so many business people have high blood pressure! Strokes are not caused by business pressures, they're caused by inane interruptions.

Despite the selfishness of the intruders, we, too, operate on a false assumption. Ours is that, despite their selfishness, we cannot be blunt and sound inhospitable or ungracious. We usually just grit our teeth and resent them later. It's not a very healthy situation.

There is a place for courtesy, but courtesy does not have to extend carte blanche to callers who interrupt the flow of thoughts, destroy concentration, or impede the continuity of effort. As a professional salesperson with limited time and unlimited work, you need to cultivate a direct, diplomatic way of handling interruptions.

The Telephone Interruption

There are two ways to control the intrusion of telephone calls—a skilled secretary or an answering machine. An answering machine simply postpones the call and puts it in your hands to be returned. (Making outgoing calls will be covered in a moment.) Having a skilled secretary is the most efficient method and should be used if possible. You will have to communicate effectively with your secretary to determine the procedures for the four different kinds of calls you'll receive.

1. *Directing traffic.* Your secretary's first duty is to determine the urgency of the call and to whom it can be referred. Many calls can be handled by others or by your secretary.

2. *Automatic call-back.* Some calls can be handled only by you but are not sufficiently urgent to warrant an interruption. Your secretary can ask the caller "May he call you back when he is free?", or better yet, "Can you call again later?" The automatic call-back is a highly effective way to avoid intrusions.

3. *Brief interruption.* Sometimes your secretary can be helpful to you and your caller. By putting the caller on hold and

asking you for a brief response to a quick question, you are saved the trouble of calling back later and the caller is satisfied.

4. *Urgent, interrupt immediately!* There will always be calls that you will predesignate as warranting an interruption. These you can handle on the spot. Hopefully, few of your daily calls fall into this category.

The Call-Back System

Now that your secretary has headed off the onslaught of calls, you have the burden of returning some of them. Unlike correspondence, calls should not be left to ripen. Create a system for returning calls which includes time-saving habits such as:

1. Determine the time of day to return calls. You may want to choose the late morning or late afternoon. At these times, chances are greater that you'll catch the other party facing lunch engagements or leaving for the day. These time pressures will make him less likely to socialize on the phone!

2. Returning calls gives the caller the chance to solve her problem on her own. Sometimes a caller will seek other sources for answering the question that she called about.

3. Information can be prepared in advance when you use the call-back system. Your secretary can pull files and gather documents which you'll need to answer the client's questions. This is obviously a time saver for you.

Outgoing Calls

The telephone is, of course, one of life's greatest time savers. It saves time over writing letters, making trips, and meeting with people. It can also be a great time waster. To avoid spending more time than necessary in calling people back, add these suggestions to the ones covered under "Call-Back System."

1. Curtail the length of your calls. This may seem obvious, but how can you do it? One effective way is to choose your opening. Don't say, "Hi, Tom, how are you?" You may be opening a can of worms. You're better off saying, "Hi,

Tom, I need to ask you a few quick questions if you have a minute." Then launch into the questions as soon as you get the OK. It's also important to be able to terminate your calls promptly. Be decisive and say, "I guess that covers it, Tom, thanks for your time, speak to you soon, goodbye." If you carry on business conversations succinctly, perhaps people will realize you are a busy person and will not waste your time when they call you.

2. Be organized. List the questions or topics you wish to discuss and have them in front of you. There's nothing worse than saying, "Uh, I forgot the other question I was going to ask you. . ." if you lose your train of thought.

3. Group your calls by type. If you are making sales calls, make them all at once. This will give you the advantage of the momentum of a mind set. You'll be in a certain thinking mode and won't have to "change gears" for every other call.

VISITORS

Visitors have the same effect as telephone calls. Again, the ideal situation is to have a secretary run interference for you. This must be done in a professional, diplomatic way.

1. Authorize your secretary to handle appointments and give her or him the authority to screen visitors also. If in doubt, your secretary can set up tentative appointments subject to your approval.

2. Set fixed "visiting" hours. You can't be receptive to visitors all day, just as a surgeon cannot have visitors in the operating room. Have your secretary tell people who "drop by" that you are busy with a patient.

3. During appointments, have your secretary monitor the visit. If it goes on for longer than normal, she can call or come in to tell you about an obligation you must attend to. You then have an easy way to terminate the meeting if necessary.

4. Block all interruptions when you have visitors. You can't talk to someone in your office and receive phone calls simultaneously.

5. Try not to socialize during business visits. Impress your visitor with how busy you are and hope he gets the hint.

6. Terminate your visits by standing up. This is an obvious sign that it's time to go. Walk your visitor to the door and say goodbye without standing by the door or elevator chatting. Unless, of course, you want to.

RELAXATION AND STRESS REDUCTION

In our goal-oriented, hyper-motivated, money-making workday we often deny ourselves the much needed periods of relaxation. Like a high-powered sports car, we can be very impressive at high speeds but sacrifice distance, efficiency, and physical integrity in the process. Our bodies and minds are designed to work well if they are not overtaxed. Frequent periods of relaxation and stress reduction are important to the longevity of our bodies and minds.

All too often the sacred coffee break is abused rather than maximized. People become focused on the process rather than the desired result of the break. A coffee or lunch break should be used as a time to relax so that you are more effective when you return to work. The relaxation you seek during a break should achieve three things:

1. It should provide distraction. You should get your mind off the job and preferably into the wild blue yonder. You'll feel much more refreshed when you land again.

2. It should alleviate tension. Our jobs often produce stiffness in the lower back, neck, and abdomen. You could do some physical activity or relaxation exercises to relieve these tensions. Many people have changed their habits in recent years. They are no longer rushing through a big meal at the lunch counter or restaurant. Instead many people go for a run, swim, play basketball, walk, or simply relax in their offices.

3. It should be short enough not to severely interfere with your workday but long enough to provide you with some benefits.

There is no denying the importance of relaxation, despite its being "unproductive." As John Wanamaker once said, "Those who do not take time for relaxation are obliged sooner or later to find time for illness."

Change Your Bad Habits

"Habit, my friend, is practice long pursued, that at the last becomes the man himself" (Evenus, 5th c. B.C.).

Managing your time efficiently and effectively will require some changes in your behavior and thinking. Those changes require *practice.* As with goals, in order to practice you must first become aware of your needs and define those you will attend to first. You have already done this. You are now much closer to effecting change in yourself than you ever were.

Giant strides, when looked at closely, are made up of many small steps. In "overhauling" your management of time, you, too, need to take small steps. We would like you to choose one area that you would like to improve. It could be procrastination, delegation, or relaxation. It's your choice—but select one now. Take the time to fill out the Time Management Key Idea Action Plan. Answer all the questions thoroughly so that you can devise a solid goal and some action steps. Start today doing those things that will make you a better manager of your time. After you've improved in one area, choose another and use the Key Idea Action Plan to define the steps. In this way, you will practice the necessary activities that will later be your good habits. Time is like money. Unless you have more than you know what to do with, you'll want to control your assets yourself. Think of time as money and you'll find yourself wasting less of it.

TIME MANAGEMENT
KEY IDEA ACTION PLAN

What is the idea I would like to implement?

What are the potential obstacles that stand in my way?

Why do I want to implement this idea? What's in it for me?

What is my action plan? How will I specifically implement the idea?

What is my target date/deadline for implementing the idea?

How and when will I measure my success?

five

Territory Management

The ingredients which most significantly affect your success as a professional salesperson are your *sales planning* and *territory management*. You may have a flawless presentation, excellent communication skills and comprehensive product knowledge. If you're presenting your product to the wrong people, however, you might as well be selling one-legged pantyhose. Effective territory management ensures that your words will fall on the right ears and have the greatest possible effect, so that your time will be well spent.

Territory management is needed for many reasons. The most obvious reason is to reduce the inefficiency of going out into the field and making random calls. Random calling may work in telephone sales where a large number of prospects can be called in a short period of time. It will not work in the field.

Over the years the cost of doing business has increased for everyone, including salespeople. Research has shown that the cost of sales calls doubled every 10 years during the last 20 years. In addition, the amount of time that a salesperson spends with a client has diminished. These two factors taken together add up to one thing—an increase in the cost of your selling time.

Inflation has also taken its toll on profit margins over the years. As profit margins slowly shrink and the cost of sales calls increases, the need for increased profitability per call becomes more urgent. This can only be accomplished by becoming more efficient through sales planning and territory management.

Territory management describes the activities required to cover the relevant markets in a given geographic area. Of these activities, the sales plan forms the skeleton upon which the rest of the system is hung. It identifies problems and opportunities, establishes priorities based on profits and the value of your time, sets objectives and strategies, and provides a means of evaluating performance over a given period of time. This is the *only* way a salesperson can hope to get a firm grip on his time, territory, and income potential. The sales plan must coincide with the company's marketing plan.

THE MARKETING PLAN

A marketing plan represents the overall strategy your company uses to identify and pursue promising markets. It includes the process of deciding the company's objectives, policies, resources, and strategies. An understanding of this process is invaluable to you for two reasons. First, it will show how your company attacks an entire market with the intention of penetrating it. Second, you will see what you must do to manage your sales territory. The principles of sales planning and territory management which you will apply are the same as those used by your company. Your plans, of course, will be on a smaller scale and affect specific accounts in a particular geographic area.

THE BIRD'S EYE VIEW

For each product manufactured or distributed, a company must determine the following:

1. *Who* and *where* are the buyers? In other words, what are the *target markets*? If a company manufactures Barbie Dolls, it certainly won't try to sell them to corporate executives (well, at least not to most of them).

2. *How* do we get to the buyers? What is the most effective way of letting the target know that the product exists? Is TV advertising, direct mail, or trade association participation most appropriate?

3. *When* is the best time to present your product to the target market? If it is a seasonal product, this will have an effect on sales planning. For example, you wouldn't want to sell wool sweaters in the summer *unless* there was something irresistible about them such as a very low price.

4. *How much* will the buyers pay? This must be looked at in absolute terms as well as in comparison to competitors' pricing.

5. *Where* and *how* will the buyers purchase the product? Will credit be extended? Can the items be leased? How will the distribution be handled?

6. Is the customer satisfied after the purchase? Did the product satisfy his needs? What kind of service will be needed in the future?

In order to answer these crucial questions, a great deal of planning and research is needed. Marketing specialists compile enough data to guide them in forecasting potential sales, setting goals and action steps, and recording the results. These plans are then passed on to other levels within the corporation for execution and evaluation. The market plan usually breaks down into four sections: Situation Analysis, Objectives, Strategy, and Control. Let's look at how this applies to the sales plan.

THE SALES PLANNING MODEL

The sales plan is practically identical to the market plan except that it deals only with one salesperson's territory rather than an entire market. If you think of your territory as a sub-market, you will see that you must perform many of the same steps as your company does in its market plan. The sales plan involves a two-stage planning process. The first stage revolves around the territory and all its characteristics. The second stage is concerned with the individual accounts and the strategies for selling them. Figure 5-1 depicts the layout of the sales plan.

Figure 5-1.   Two-stage sales planning project.

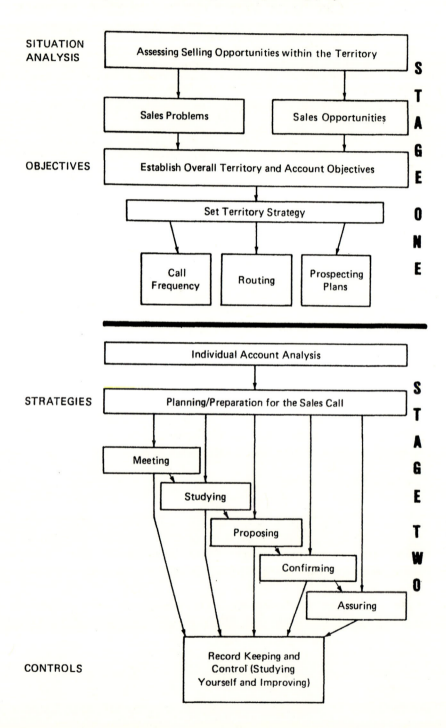

In the first stage, assess your selling opportunities and problems just as the market plan does. In your search for exploitable sales opportunities, study the following:

Step 1:

1. Your company and its products or services.
2. The industry in general.
3. The competition and their market penetration.
4. The market potential in your territory.
5. Business trends in different market segments.

From this analysis you can set some realistic territory and sales objectives. These goals would center around the following:

Step 2:

*   The most profitable products or services to be sold.
*   The accounts of weak competitors to be pursued.
*   Prime market segments in your entire territory.
*   Groups of specific prospects to be contacted.
*   Objectives of total sales or volume for your entire territory and individual accounts.

Step 3 involves developing strategies to accomplish the objectives you've set out. These strategies will include time (Chapter 4) and territory management. Territory management strategies include elements such as the frequency and priority of calls, methods of contacting, promotional aids (to be covered in Chapter 7) and prospecting plans (Chapter 6). After all of this territory research has been completed, you can then move on to the second stage.

Specific accounts are dealt with in Step 4. Here the sales opportunities and strategies are analyzed on an account-by-account basis, giving special attention to the following:

1. Prospect's purchasing behavior and needs.
2. Characteristics of the prospect's company.
3. Overall industry the prospect is in.
4. Actual or potential competition.

This research will uncover a wealth of information which can be used to great advantage when contacting a prospect or pre-existing customer. Naturally, sales and call objectives will be set for each account. These are both long term and per-call goals. They can be as long-range as "sell $100,000 worth of product X in the next year" or as short-range as "introduce product at first meeting and schedule a demonstration."

The sixth step is the actual sales call itself. This involves meeting with the prospect or client, studying her needs, proposing solutions, confirming the sale, and assuring that the benefits will be effective solutions to her problems.

Last, but not least in the sales plan, is the control phase. This is a nice way of saying that you'll be required to keep records of what you have done so that you can evaluate your performance later. Without the data provided by records, you will have no way of knowing if you accomplished your goals for the territory or individual accounts. Without this feedback you will not be able to correct whatever problems you are having in achieving your objectives.

The two-stage planning process is a closed-loop system in which all stages depend upon each other. All the information obtained in the control section is "fed back" to the situation analysis so that the process can begin again. This is a cycle that every *successful* salesperson goes through on a yearly or semiannual basis. The time taken to carefully plan the strategies for a given period of time will pay off in increased sales and increased awareness of what is being done correctly or incorrectly. This will turn the art of selling into a science for you.

SITUATION ANALYSIS

Today's business climate is in constant flux, changing from week to week with the whims of a capricious economy. These rapid changes necessitate periodic assessments of the sales territory. The systematic and exhaustive assessment of sales problems and opportunities will arm you with the knowledge necessary to maximize your time and efficiency.

COMPANY KNOWLEDGE

Your company is the only entity which stands behind the product or service you are selling. Initially, customers may be more interested in your company than in you and the product. You must be knowledgeable enough to educate your client if you want to gain her trust and confidence.

Company knowledge is independent of product knowledge. You need to be familiar with the history and development of both. If you are a sales rep carrying many products, becoming familiar with each company may seem like an arduous task. It should, however, be done conscientiously. The Company/Product Knowledge worksheet on the following page will test your knowledge and guide you in acquiring the facts you should know about your company and product(s).

Often a company will describe their history, development, and philosophy when you begin working for them. If they do not, you can approach marketing or sales managers and ask them for the information. The same is true for product knowledge. If there are gaps in the information your company has given you, seek out the knowledgeable people and tell them your needs. Often engineers, executives, and others in high-level positions know more than those who sell the products. You should also be aware of your company's operating activities. Is it buying new subsidiaries or creating new divisions? How well is its stock doing on the market? Have there been any significant managerial or executive changes lately? If so, how will this affect the company's policies? All of these things are worth knowing so that a customer will not embarrass you by asking a question you cannot answer. Your knowledge will indicate to your client that you care about your firm and that you do business in a professional manner.

PRODUCT KNOWLEDGE

Every company provides its salespeople with information about the product they will sell. This takes the form of brochures, specification sheets, and other printed materials. In addition, many companies offer training sessions, workshops, and other informative classes to bring their people up to date on the latest development in their products. All of this is extremely valuable and should be absorbed voraciously by the salesperson.

As technology develops at phenomenal rates, product cycles become shorter and shorter. What is new today is obsolete tomorrow. More often than not, the salesperson knows more than her customers about these changes. It is necessary, therefore, for the

Worksheet 5-A
Company/Product Knowledge

INSTRUCTIONS: Answer all of the questions below in as much detail as possible. Questions which you cannot answer will point out areas that you need to research.

COMPANY

1. List the key personnel of your company and what their unique contribution to the firm is.

2. What unique capabilities or technical advantages does the company have?

3. What is the company's image and reputation among: a) Present customers b) Prospects c) The competition.

4. What are the relative strengths and weaknesses compared to the competition? How do these affect business?

5. What is the marketing philosophy of your company?

6. What are the present and future markets of your company?

7. What has the company's sales history been during the last 3-5 years?

8. What is your company's standard policy regarding: a) Pricing b) Discounts c) Guarantees d) Service.

PRODUCT

1. What specific benefits do present and prospective customers seek in your product?

2. How does your product compare to the competition's in providing those benefits?

3. Are there any features which make your product better than the competition's? If so, why?

4. How does your product compare to the others in your territory in the following aspects: a) Quality b) Price c) Deliver d) Value e) Reliability

5. What factor(s) might prevent a customer from purchasing a product? What can you do about it?

6. Is your company a leader (developer) or follower (imitator) in its field?

salesperson to introduce product changes to a customer in a way which will be informative as well as attractive. The growing need for salespeople to keep abreast of industrial changes is illustrated by the fact that salespeople in the digital watch, calculator, and video game industries spend as much as 50 percent of their time just learning about their products!

As mentioned before, some sales representatives carry more than one product. For them, the task of organizing their products and becoming knowledgeable about each is made more difficult by a factor of "n" (n = the number of product lines carried). If a salesperson carries three lines, it is three times as much work to know all those products. To help organize one's knowledge, a Multi-Product Knowledge worksheet is presented. This aid will uncover what you know and what you need to research further. It will also shed light on any product weaknesses you might not have recognized.

MARKET ANALYSIS

Knowing your own company and products is only part of the battle. You must also know the market of which your territory is a small part. An analysis of your territory by *market segments* will simplify the process. A market segment is one category or type of industry or business. For example, if you are selling copying machines, some of the market segments would be banks, libraries, hospitals, law firms, doctor's offices, and so on. Each of these segments will be different but, within each category, the individual account's needs will be quite similar.

For each of your market segments you will want to know the potential demand for your product in terms of gross sales and number of units to be sold. This *quantitative* analysis will be done for a specified period of time, usually one year. Two types of data are needed for an accurate market analysis—*market potential* and *sales potential*. Market potential comprises the maximum sales possible for all companies in the market. For example, how many copying machines will be sold in your territory regardless of manufacturer? Sales potential data seeks to determine the maximum sales potential for a specific company during a given period of time.

You will be interested in the sales potential in your territory for each of your market segments. This will help you in many ways.

Worksheet 5-B
Multi-Product Knowledge Worksheet

Product knowledge for _____ as of _____
                    (your company)   (date)

Please answer Yes or No to
the following questions:

PRODUCTS

	1.	2.	3.	4.	5.
Can you describe the benefits, features and advantages?					
Do you know all the applications of this product?					
Can you explain the company's marketing plan and rationale?					
Can you describe how it relates to other products?					
Do you know its competitive position?					
Can this product be used with others to solve a client's problems?					
Can you project the financial benefits to be derived by the client? From this product?					

First, you will see at a glance which market segments appear to be most promising. You'll be able to rank the market segments in order of priority and budget your time accordingly. Second, seeing the relative fertility of different market segments, you'll be able to set different (and therefore more realistic) objectives for each, as well as different amounts of money for promotion and personal selling efforts.

To determine the make-up of your territory, you should divide it into segments. This is done by listing all possible uses of your product and the industries or businesses who will use it.

First, you must determine the number, location, and sales potential of each customer or prospect. This compilation will take research and creativity on your part. Be as thorough as possible. Names of present customers can be obtained from your company, other sales people, or your own files. Prospects can be identified with the aid of trade directories (e.g., Thomas' Register), publishers of mailing lists (e.g., R. H. Donnelley Corp.), and other journals, magazines, and firms (e.g., Dunn & Bradstreet).

After the customers are listed, make an assessment of the potential business from each.

This is done by examining their past sales records, if available. For prospect's estimates, the same sources mentioned can be used. After forecasts are made for each company, they should be ranked in order of their potential profitability.

MARKET TRENDS

During this phase you should also be aware of any situations that may be affecting business. These can range from economic to political changes. For example, everyone is aware of the effect of interest rates on the economy. This is a trend worth considering when forecasting sales. The sooner you recognize a trend and figure it into your analysis, the better off you'll be. Trends usually suggest areas of caution or opportunities to be exploited. Being an aware, well-read salesperson is one of the best ways to get a jump on business trends.

COMPETITION ANALYSIS

There are very few products or services with no direct competitors. We need to be aware of competition.

An important part of your territory analysis will be the evaluation of competitors. You will want to identify all those who have a significant influence on the market segments you are interested in. Analyze their share of the market, their strengths and weaknesses, and where they are headed in the future. The two worksheets (5-C and 5-D) that follow will help you organize your findings and rank your competitors on two criteria—their company/product strengths and weaknesses and their positioning/penetration in each target market segment.

Worksheet 5-C compares your company to the competition in eight areas of criteria important to your customers. Feel free to add as many criteria as you wish to the list. To complete Worksheet 5-C you simply need to rank your company *objectively* against the major competitors on *each* of the customer decision criteria (No. 1 is the highest ranking company for each criterion).

From this worksheet, you will quickly see which areas need improving and which can be emphasized in your selling efforts. For example, if your company is strong in pricing but weak in delivery, you should do what you can to improve delivery and emphasize pricing as a selling point. By knowing which competitor is highest in customer service, you'll know who to study so that your sales can increase.

Worksheet 5-D compares competitors' strengths in different market segments. This information is extremely valuable. Let's say, for example, that one market segment seems to be neglected by practically all of your competitors. This could be a golden opportunity for you to penetrate a new market! You would, of course, find out why the others are not well represented in that market segment. It is possible that a particular segment is not profitable for a number of reasons. If this is the case, you have a good reason not to pursue it. This determination requires more research but is well worth the effort.

In Worksheet 5-D you should again objectively rank each company on either its market share or its relative strength in *each* of the market segments you've identified. (Use the same 10-point scale as you used in Worksheet 5-C.)

It is not enough to fill in the table and simply observe the standings of your company and its competitors. You must find out *why* these standings exist as they are. Then answer the next

Worksheet 5-C
Competition Analysis Matrix

	Your Company	COMPETITORS			
		A	B	C	D
CUSTOMER DECISION CRITERIA Sales					
Reputation					
Pricing					
Quality Products					
Customer Service					
Market Share					
Growth Rate					
Financial Strength					

question: *How* can these standings be changed so that my company gets a bigger share next year in the segments we would like to penetrate?

After you've analyzed the competition and the various market segments, take a look at the factors which influence sales in each segment. This will show you which decision criteria can be emphasized for increased sales in each individual segment. The information for this analysis will have to come from the customers themselves. Survey the businesses or industries within the market segments to uncover their satisfactions and dissatisfactions. Worksheet 5-E can be used to organize your evaluation of this data and suggest opportunities to be pursued by you.

Worksheet 5-E, in showing you the decision-making criteria for different segments, will help steer you towards a market which will capitalize on the strengths of your company and product. For example, if you sell an expensive but very reliable copying machine, you will want to know which market segment values reliability over purchase price. In your research you might find that banks and stationers buy those brands that are reliable. On the other hand, you may find law firms spending less for less reliable machines. Worksheets 5-C and 5-E will give you a good feel for your territory and what you have to do to penetrate it further strategically.

CUSTOMER INFORMATION

Now that you have some idea of the market segments you will go after, you need to learn more about the individual accounts. The first step is to list all the major customers and prospects in your territory for each market segment. By now you have done enough research to have uncovered the major clients. You may have to stretch your imagination and devote more time to finding specific prospects. Take the time to do this. As we will discuss in the following chapter, your need for prospects is continual. To organize your client and prospect list, we have included Worksheet 5-F for you to use. Fill out a worksheet for every product and every market segment you sell to. At this point the order is unimportant. After you've further analyzed each prospect, you will go back and list your customers in order of priority.

Worksheet 5-D
Competitors' Market Share Worksheet

	Your Company	COMPETITORS			
		A	B	C	D
M A R K E T S E G M E N T S	I (Lawyers)*				
	II (Banks)				
	III (Retailers)				
	etc.				

*These categories are used only as examples Please fill in all market segments relative to your own product or service.

Worksheet 5-E
Market Segment Needs Worksheet

| | | MARKET SEGMENTS* | | |
	I	II	III	IV
Reputation				
Pricing				
Delivery				
Quality				
Customer Service				
Financial Strength				
Etc.				

(left vertical label: CUSTOMER DECISION CRITERIA)

*From Worksheet 5—D

INSTRUCTIONS: Rank (1—10) which factors are most important to each market segment in their decision to purchase a product or service like yours.

Worksheet 5-F
Market Segment Breakdown

MARKET SEGMENT _____ Product(s) _____ Date _____

CUSTOMERS/CLIENTS

PROSPECTS

Although prospecting will be covered in the following chapter, it is appropriate to discuss some sources of prospects here. These sources will also provide invaluable financial and organizational information to be used in the individual account analyses which will follow. The following sources represent only a fraction of the available information on industry and business. For more references, see your local reference librarian.

Sources of Information/Prospects

- Standard & Poor's Industry Surveys
- Forbes Annual Report on Business
- Moody's Industrial Manual
- Dunn & Bradstreet Reference Book of Corporate Management.
- Standard & Poor's Corporate Record
- Encyclopedia of Business Information Sources
- Periodicals
- Government Publications from
  - U. S. Dept. of Commerce
  - U. S. Treasury Dept. (IRS)
  - Bureau of Census
  - Bureau of Economic Analysis
  - Dept. of Labor
- Funk & Scott Index of Corporations and Industries
- Wall Street Transcript
- Newspapers, Trade Journals, Periodicals
- Consulting Firms
- Annual Reports, stock prospectuses, stock performance guides
- Personal Contacts
- Company's resources, other sales people, etc.
- Trade Associations

Sources are so numerous that there is never an excuse for being short of prospects. While doing your research, gather as much information as you can, but keep it relevant. To accomplish this, you need to know what is involved in the analysis of your accounts and prospects.

ACCOUNT ANALYSIS

You've spent hours researching and analyzing, but what has it all been for? In one word—*Priorities*! It takes knowledge to decide what to do and when to do it, or, in your case, *who* to call on and *when*. The analysis of each account and prospect will show you in hard figures which calls are worth your time and effort and which are not.

If you remember Pareto's 80-20 principle, you'll see that 20 percent of your accounts constitute 80 percent of your total sales. The sales expenses for these key accounts are not much greater than for the smaller, less profitable accounts. For this reason you must identify and cater to the profitable 20 percent and make them grow. This is the beginning of setting your account priorities.

To set your priorities, it is necessary to look at your customers from two points of view. First, what will each account contribute to your overall sales profit? Second, what is the time investment necessary to cover that account and realize the profit potential? An important part of this second analysis is to determine what your time is worth on an hourly basis. The profitability of an account can be determined only if you have an idea of the overhead costs of your product. This cost includes your time as a salesperson.

There are several reasons why few salespeople analyze and classify their accounts. As people, we all tend to be lazy. We also tend to call on people who are pleasant to deal with even if their profitability as accounts is low. It feels good to have a warm chat with a client on a cold day. (Cold chats on warm days can be refreshing too!) Another reason is that salespeople prefer to sell products that are easy to move rather than the more profitable, slower moving ones. This is in part due to the fact that most of us feel more rewarded by short-term commissions than by long-term commissions. Most people focus on the short term in their planning. The classification and prioritization of accounts requires a long-term outlook and a desire to build accounts over time. The rewards are eventually greater for those who can forego the short-term gratification in favor of the bigger long-term rewards.

ACCOUNT CLASSIFICATION

The first step in classifying your accounts is to divide them into market segments. From these lists, take each account and analyze it on its own merits. The procedure is to make up an account profile; determine the profit margin; and estimate the cost of your time, the volume necessary to break even, and the return of your invested time. This will all lead to a rating of the account as an A, B, or C (high, medium, low) account. You will then be able to determine how much time to spend with each account based on its expected return.

It should be noted that your accounts can be classified in terms of sales volume. This is not, however, the most efficient way. Sales volume is a one-dimensional measure which hides half the truth. It is entirely plausible that you may have customers who are high in volume yet low in profitability. It could be that your expenses in reaching these customers are so high that your profit margin is cut significantly. In this case, ranking them as highly desirable or "A" accounts would be economically unsound. We advocate the use of profitability as a yardstick of the account's worth/value.

ACCOUNT PROFILE

Your "bible" for each account will be the account profile. This is the Worksheet 5-G on which you will enter all information you find during your research and analysis phases. The profile will be a permanent record to be used to refresh your memory about everything from sales volume to the buyer's name and personal style. Enter whatever information you feel is relevant to the account. We have presented a sample account profile on the following pages. Use ours as a starting point to design and duplicate your own for each account and prospect you will have. In doing so, remember to leave lots of space for new information.

As you can see on the profile, much of the information is straightforward. One of the first places to improvise on your own profiles is under the buyer's name(s). Here you can list little reminders such as personal style, best time of day to call, spouse's name, and so on. These things will help you add a personal touch to the sales call.

Some of the information will be unavailable to you if the profile is for a prospect rather than the current customer. Our primary concern now is with existing accounts and the determination of their profitability. Under profitability analysis is a space for profit margin. This figure comes from one of two sources. If you are in direct sales for a company like Avon, Amway, or Shaklee, then you know what the product costs you and what you sell it for. The difference is your gross profit margin. If you work for a company and are not told what the profit margin is, you can find out by asking an executive in the accounting or marketing department. The number of calls and time per call will be obtained from your past records (What do you mean, you don't keep any?). This is also true of your travel and planning time for each account as well.

The rest of the account profile is devoted to the calculations necessary for classifying the account as an A, B, or C. We will begin with the value of your time. This can be determined in two ways, both useful.

Cost Per Hour

The cost method of deriving your time's worth takes into consideration the direct costs accrued in your pursuit of an account. These direct costs include your salary, bonuses, commissions, travel expenses, and other miscellaneous expenses. Knowing the profit margin of the product is not necessary to figure your cost per hour (CPH). The formula is

$$CPH = \frac{DC}{WH}$$

where CPH = Cost per hour
DC = Direct costs
WH = Working hours

For example, let's say a salesperson's direct costs are

Salary	$ 15,000
Commissions	3,000
Travel	8,000
Miscellaneous	4,000
Direct Costs	$ 30,000

Worksheet 5-G
Account Profile

Company Name: _____

Street Address: _____

City/State/Zip: _____

Telephone: _____

Buyers (in order of importance): _____

_____

Products/Services Purchased: _____

_____

Buying Characteristics:

When Does Customer Buy? _____

How Often? _____ Average Order/Call: _____

Gross Sales Volume (yearly): _____

Past Sales (last 4 yrs.): _____

_____

_____

Company Goals:

    Short Term (as perceived?): _____

_____

    Long Term (as perceived by?): _____

_____

Competitors (for this account):

    Current Competitors: _____

_____

    Potential Competitors: _____

_____

Worksheet 5-G
Account Profile

Your Company/product strengths: _____

_____

_____

Your Company/product weaknesses: _____

_____

_____

Your Goals for Acct. _____ as of (date) _____

_____

_____

Specific Account Needs:

_____ Pricing _____ Delivery _____ Service

_____ Credit _____ Reliability _____ Other ( )

PROFITABILITY ANALYSIS

Profit Margin _____ Margin Percentage (GMP) _____

Number of calls necessary/year: _____

Average time per call: _____

Travel time per call: _____

Planning time per call: _____

Your Cost per Hour (CPH): _____ $CPH = \dfrac{DC}{WH}$

Your Cost per Call Hour (CPCH): _____ $CPCH = \dfrac{DC}{CH}$

Break-even Volume: _____ $BEV = \dfrac{DC}{GMP}$

Break-even Volume/Call: _____ $BEV/hr. = \dfrac{CPCH}{GMP}$ call

Return of Time Invested: _____ $ROTI = \dfrac{GM}{DC}$ $CTI = DC$

Account Classification: _____

This is fairly typical because direct costs are usually twice the salesperson's salary. To figure cost per hour (*CPH*), you then divide the figure representing direct costs by 2,000 working hours (based on 40 hours per week for 50 weeks of the year) (if your working hours differ from our figure, please use your own figures):

$$CPH = \frac{DC}{WH} = \frac{\$\ 30,000}{2,000} = \$15/hr.$$

In this example, the salesperson's time is worth $15.00 per hour. This is not terribly accurate, however, because none of us are fully productive for 40 hours a week. It's nice to think we're being paid while we eat lunch, but in reality it's just not so. It's much more accurate to assume that your "call hours" are the only productive hours in your day. To know what your time is worth during the sales call (and later to determine whether you're wasting time or not), you need to divide your direct costs by the number of call hours (CH) in a year rather than the total hours worked.

$$\text{Cost Per Call Hour } (CPCH) = \frac{DC}{CH} = \frac{\$\ 30,000}{800} = \$37.50/hr.$$

The cost per call hour is important to keep in mind so that you can aspire to earn more money per call hour than you cost your company. Doing so will put you in the black rather than in the red or simply breaking even.

Break-even Sales Volume

Now that you know what your time is worth per call hour, you can figure out how much you have to sell in order to break even. In calculating your break-even volume, you must know the gross margin on your products. We'll assume you either know or can find out this information. For the purpose of illustration, let's use the case of a salesperson getting a product for one price and selling it for another. The difference will be the gross profit margin. The formula for calculating break-even volume is

$$BEV = \frac{DC}{GMP}$$

where *BEV* = Break-even Volume
DC = Direct Costs
GMP = Gross Margin Percentage

Let's say a salesperson has gross sales of $100,000 in a year and the product sold cost $80,000. Subtracting the latter from the former would give you the gross profit. This will also be expressed in a percentage of the gross sales.

Sales $100,000
Cost of Product   −   80,000
Gross Profit $ 20,000
Gross Margin Percentage   *(GMP)* = $\frac{\$\ 20,000}{\$100,000}$ = .2 or 20%

From this, the break-even volume can be calculated:

$$BEV = \frac{DC}{GMP} = \frac{\$\ 30,000}{.20} = \$150,000$$

This figure tells you what your sales volume must be for the year in order to cover your direct costs and simply break even. Naturally you will aim to have gross sales far above your break-even volume so that you can contribute to the profits of your company (and be indispensable as a salesperson).

Knowing what your volume has to be for the year doesn't give you a feel for how you're doing on a per-call-hour basis. This can be worked out by the following formula:

$$BEV/\text{call hour} = \frac{CPCH}{GMP}$$

As in the examples above, if your sales call time is worth $37.50/hr. and your gross margin percentage is 20%, your break-even volume per call hour is

$$BEV/\text{call hour} = \frac{\$37.50}{.20} = \$187.50$$

This tells you that for every hour you make sales calls (based on 800 call hours/year), you need to make $187.50 in sales in order to just break even.

Now that you know what your time is worth, you are much closer to making an objective evaluation of whether a particular account is worth your time to call on.

Return On Time Invested

The final step in evaluating an account before assigning it a priority is calculating your Return on Time Invested (ROTI). This is basically a ratio of the results of your efforts to the amount of effort you put in.

$$ROTI = \frac{\text{Sales results}}{\text{Sales efforts}}$$

As in the value of your time, in ROTI there are several ways of measuring sales results and effort. Sales results can be measured in gross margin, gross sales, or number of units sold. The best method is to use gross margin, which we have available to us already. Sales effort can be measured in the number of calls, amount of time spent on the account, or the direct cost of your time. Since we've been working with direct cost, we should continue to do so. The formula looks like this:

$$ROTI = \frac{GM}{DC}$$ where $ROTI$ = Return on Time Invested
GM = Gross Margin in $
DC = Direct Costs in $

Let's say a salesperson has gross sales of $30,000 in a year to Account A and knows her gross margin percentage is 20%. From this we can calculate her gross margin:

GM = Sales Volume x GMP = $30,000 x .20 = $6,000.

The question still remains: Was the account worth her time? She projects her direct costs for Account A to be $3,000. So, from a quick glance we can see she earned $3,000. This can also be expressed in a ratio as ROTI:

$$ROTI = \frac{GM}{DC} = \frac{\$\ 6,000}{\$\ 3,000} = 2$$

The number *2* indicates that her return on time invested on Account A was two to one. Ratios provide a faster means of comparison than straight profit figures. The ROTI ratio takes into account both the factors of profit and time invested. It, therefore, keeps everything in the perspective we want. A ratio greater than one is profitable. A ratio of one means breaking even and a ratio of less than one means a loss, because more money was spent in costs than made in profits for that account.

The Point of It All—Account Classification

The last item on your account profile is the account classification based on your past ROTI. After you have calculated your ROTI's for all your accounts, you should divide them into three groups. The highest 20% or so could be designated "A" accounts. These are the most worthwhile customers in terms of profitability. The middle 50% might be designated "B" accounts, and the bottom 30% classified as "C" accounts. You may want to use your own percentage breakdowns for A, B, and C Accounts based on the specific ROTI scores your accounts generate.

To further help you organize your classified accounts, we have provided worksheet 5-H on which to list them. The Key Account Worksheet simply categorizes the accounts so that you can see them all in front of you.

Another interesting way of organizing your client list is shown in the grid of Worksheet 5-I. This compares customers in terms of profit (ROTI) and sales volume. Evaluate each of your accounts in these areas and write their names in the appropriate squares. From this you will see which accounts require profit improvement and which require volume improvement, or both. For example, you will try to increase volume for those accounts which fall into the high-profit, low-volume area (upper left). For low-profit, low-volume accounts (lower left), you will try to increase both (without spending too much time on them because they would be considered poor "C" accounts). The difficult combination to improve is the high-volume, low-profit accounts. In this case, it is either the profit margin of the product that needs to be changed or the direct costs. Unless you are inefficient, it is difficult to significantly lower your overhead. You might be better off trying to improve other accounts in the grid, keeping in mind that the desired direction of the improvement is up from the lower left and across to the right side of the grid.

Having analyzed and classified your accounts into A's, B's, and C's, you can now take a look at the problems and opportunities in your territory. This will suggest objectives and strategies for dealing with them.

Worksheet 5-H
Key Account Worksheet

DATE:_____ through_____

Product/Service: _____

_____"A" Accounts_____

_____"B" Accounts_____

_____"C" Accounts_____

_____Prospects_____

Worksheet 5-I
Categorization of Accounts by Volume and Profit

SALES VOLUME

	Low	Med.	High
High			
Med.			
Low			

R
E
T
U
R
N

O
N

T
I
M
E

I
N
V
E
S
T
E
D

TERRITORY PROBLEMS AND OPPORTUNITIES

Our world is in a constant state of flux. Changes in every facet of life occur so quickly that you'd need a computer to keep track of them all. The business world is no different. Changes in manufacturing, commercial, and retail enterprises seem to be almost mercurial. As a professional salesperson, you need to keep pace with the changes in your territory. Some of these changes will be to your advantage and others will cause headaches. The more aware you are, however, the fewer headaches they will cause.

Opportunities and problems can arise from both inside and outside the company. Environmental and market influences can affect sales as much as company policies, products, or services. Factors in the market which may cause increased opportunities include changes in consumer demand, fads, increased affluence due to social mobility, and the increased impact of technology. In fact, technology is such a strong influence on products that manufacturers estimate that over half of their existing products have been on the market for less than five years. This, obviously, will affect the salespeople handling those products.

Opportunities that stem from your company are the easiest to define and take advantage of. In your competition analysis you should have listed those strengths which put your company and its products ahead of your competitors. These can create strong selling points in market segments which will respond to them. Your company can also create opportunities through the introduction of new products or the improvement of old ones. New features and benefits often create renewed interest and sales. Promotional specials accomplish the same purpose by offering your customers a one-time-only offer which they can't refuse.

Every market segment and company has its problems. There's no denying that some problems exist out in the field because of things the company has done. Sometimes poor management causes the company's image to be less than ideal. Often a salesperson will start working for a company which has just changed ownership and needs to overcome a bad reputation. This adds another challenge to the overall task of selling. The new reputation is built through the sales force and service, so your role is essential in this metamorphosis.

Other influences from outside the company can cause problems. Unfavorable market trends can shift business away from you. Customers can be very fickle; a change in technology or fads may trigger a switch to another company. Although changing fads can create opportunities, they can also dry up a market. Stiff competition can cause problems, and it's tough on a salesperson. There's no denying that some companies dominate a market segment; it requires an extra effort on your part to compete with them. The best way to do this is to carefully analyze your relative strengths and capitalize on them.

After completing a situation analysis for all your market segments, isolate the problems and opportunities and set up objectives for dealing with them. You cannot do this just once, however, and leave it at that. Being aware of changes is a continuing part of being a successful salesperson.

Territory Objectives

Setting objectives is the next step in the overall management of your territory. The objectives you create should flow directly from your situation analysis as well as your observations of the existing territory problems and opportunities. Naturally, these goals will be aimed at overcoming the problems and exploiting the opportunities.

There are several other reasons for setting territory objectives. First, they serve as an incentive to motivate you. Only when you are challenged sufficiently will you seek new performance levels and strive toward loftier goals. Second, objectives define and control your activities. They take the randomness out of your calls by creating priorities. Objectives suggest action to be taken. Finally, concrete objectives give you something by which to evaluate your performance. They act as yardsticks from which you can gauge your effectiveness. From this feedback you will then modify your next set of objectives.

The objectives you set for your territory should include all accounts, market segments, products and services, and promotional and travel expenses. Some examples of territory objectives are

1. Dollar volume for entire territory.
2. Percentage increase in volume over last year by certain percentage range.
3. Increase in sales of certain products by certain amounts.

4. Increase in overall sales or specific product sales in particular market segments.

5. Reduction by a certain percentage of overhead expenses for the entire territory.

6. Addition of specific market segments to the overall sales effort.

7. Increase in the number of new accounts over last year by a certain percentage.

8. Increase in total dollar sales per customer.

9. Upgrading a certain percentage of "C" accounts to "B's" and "B" accounts to "A's."

10. Seeing a certain number of prospects per week and turning a certain percentage of them into accounts.

11. Reduction in expenses of sales calls by a certain percentage.

12. Increase in the ratio of actual sales to sales calls.

13. Addition of a certain number of qualified prospects to your files per month or year.

One could go on and on listing objectives. The point is that your objectives will have to custom fit your customers, products and services, market segments, and territory. Your choice of objectives will make the difference between effective and ineffective management and sales in your territory.

Territory Strategy

Everything we do requires a strategy, no matter how simple it may be. If you are going to run an errand, you plan how you'll travel, the best route to take, and how much time to spend doing it. When you have several errands, you usually figure out the most efficient way of accomplishing them all in the shortest amount of time. This is done so that you can save money, energy, and gas and have some time left over for other activities. The same time management principle applies to territory management. Now that you have analyzed your accounts, classified them according to their profitability, and set objectives, you are in a position to decide when and how to call on them, how many to call on, and with what frequency.

There is no such thing as the "best" way to cover a territory. Every salesperson has a different combination of territory size, market segments, number of customers, and sales ability. There is, however, a general format which can be used and adapted by everyone in planning their territory strategy.

One of the first questions you need to answer is, "How many customers and prospects can I call on within the next planning period?" Our Call Frequency Planner (Worksheet 5-J) will prove invaluable to you in the analysis of this question. This is how it works:

1. Count the total number of A, B, and C accounts and prospects you wish to call on in your next planning period. In our "Call Frequency Planner" example, we're planning for the next six months. The numbers we used in the Call Frequency Planner, Column 2, are 20, 50, 20 and 10.

2. From past experience and your account profiles, determine the average number of calls that you make on your accounts in each category. If you are planning for six months, as we are, you can think in terms of visits twice a month, once a month, once every two months, or once a quarter. Column 3 lists the call frequencies for the six-month planning period.

3. Column 4 shows the total number of calls per category for the entire planning period. This figure is obtained by multiplying Column 2 by Column 3.

4. For each of your account classifications, calculate the average length of a sales call. This information should be available from your call records. The length of a call for prospects can be judged from your past experience. As a rule of thumb, the time required for a prospect's call will be the same as other accounts within that market segment because their needs are so similar. Enter these averages in Column 5.

5. The time required for a call comprises more than the actual time spent face-to-face with a customer. It also includes planning and travel time. Both of these can be calculated from your records and field experience. We have used a

travel time of 20 minutes for all types of accounts. Obviously, your numbers will be different. If your territory covers a large geographical area, you may want to fill out a separate worksheet for each area. This would prevent the differences in travel time from affecting the accuracy and realism of the planner.

6. Column 7 ask for the total time for each classification of accounts. This is simply the sum of columns 5, 6, and 7, multiplied by Column 4. For example, the total time for "A" accounts is

    Total time (Col. 8) = (40 + 30 + 20)240 = 21,600 minutes

    This tells you that for the next six months you are going to spend 21,600 minutes on your "A" accounts.

7. Column 9 converts the total time from minutes to hours. This is done by dividing the total in Column 8 by 60 minutes per hour.

8. After arriving at the total hours for each type of account, add the figures in Column 9 so that you'll know the total number of hours you'll have to work for the period. In our example, the total is 777 hours. Dividing this figure by 8 hours per day will give you the number of days required to cover all these accounts. 777 hours equals 97 days.

If you use a planning period of six months, then you have 120 days in which to work (based on five days per week). After filling out your Call Frequency Planner, if you find that your territory requires, for example, 97 days of work, then you can realistically manage your accounts in the next six months. However, if your total number of days exceeds 120, then you need to go back and readjust your Planner. You could do this in several ways:

• Plan to call on fewer accounts, especially fewer "C" and low priority "B" accounts.

• Reduce travel time.

• Use alternative methods of contacting accounts and prospects. For example, the less profitable accounts can be contacted by telephone or mail. This will save time which can then be devoted to the conversion of "B's" to "A's," and so on.

If, as in our example, you find that you have planned for fewer than 120 days, you have two choices. You can increase any of the variables that seem too small. For example, you may want to increase call time or the number of prospects called on. Whatever you do, be sure to make the adjustment with profitability in mind. Your other choice is to leave the Planner as it is and use the extra time to cover the inevitable emergencies, unexpected delays, waiting time, cancellations, and added travel time. Although you don't want too much extra time on your hands, neither do you want to create stress by planning your schedule to the exact minute.

The Call Frequency Planner, in a nutshell, lets you know if your call objectives are possible within the time allotted. Let's say one of your objectives is to add 25 new accounts in the next six months. If you know from experience that for every six prospects you call on, two become customers, then you'll have to call on 75 prospects. If you can only humanly manage to call on 300 accounts in six months, then one quarter of them will have to be prospects in order to reach this goal. You can see now how the planner puts everything into the realistic perspective of available time.

Alternatives to Personal Calls

When mapping out your territory, evaluate "B's," "C's," and prospects for possible alternatives to personal calls. Obviously the cost of a telephone call is significantly less than the cost of a personal call. If a call can be made effectively over the phone, it should be considered for all classifications of accounts. "A's," however, should be phoned only if there's absolutely no risk of alienating the customer.

In covering your territory, try alternating between phone calls and personal calls for "B" and "C" accounts. You might also try contacting "C" accounts strictly by phone and doing all your prospecting, market research, and scheduling by telephone. To augment your calls, you can send personal letters with promotional literature to all accounts. This, too, will save you time over personal calls.

CONTROL

The statistical evaluation of your sales performance forms a major tool for improving sales and lowering marketing costs. The collection and analysis of sales activity data will tell you *what* you

Worksheet 5-J
Call Frequency Planner (Sample)

1 Acct. Class	2 Number	3 Call Freq.	4 Call Total	5 Time/ Call (min)	6 Plan Time	7 Travel Time	8 Total Time	9 Hours/ Cycle
A	20	12	240	40	30	20	21,600	360
B	50	6	300	30	20	20	21,000	350
C	20	3	60	20	10	20	3,000	50
Prospect	10	2	20	20	10	20	1,000	17
Totals	100		320					777 hrs.

Number of Days = $\dfrac{777 \text{ hrs.}}{8 \text{hrs/day}}$ = 97 days

Worksheet 5-J
Call Frequency Planner

1 Acct. Class	2 Number	3 Call Freq.	4 Call Total	5 Time/ Call (min)	6 Plan Time	7 Travel Time	8 Total Time	9 Hours/ Cycle
A								
B								
C								
Prospect								
Totals:								hrs.

Number of Days = $\dfrac{hrs.}{hrs/day}$ = _____ days

are doing as well as *why*. This is the only way of discovering your strengths and weaknesses and the means to doing something about them. The control procedure allows you to stand back and see your effectiveness objectively in the same way a manager would. Control guides you to being a better salesperson in the future.

There are four phases to the control of a sales territory: standards of performance, collection of data on actual performance, performance analysis, and corrective action.

Standards of Performance

Every experiment has a baseline to which the results are compared. The standards you set up for your sales territory and individual accounts are the objectives you set up previously. These range from total sales volume for the territory to small details about one particular account. This process will lead you to the design of forms that will measure your performance both quantitatively and qualitatively.

Data Collection and Record Keeping

Paperwork is an unavoidable part of our lives. In sales, it is part of an ongoing routine which simply becomes second nature. The records you keep serve to refresh your memory, evaluate your performance, and reflect trends in account and market activities. It is important that you know what records are valuable and which are a waste of time. Develop the ability to design your own forms so that you can collect data on your personal goals and objectives. You should keep certain standard records:

Customer file. These consist of 3 × 5 cards with customer information on them—name, address, phone, buying criteria, important salespeople, customer's personal style, past sales, needs, competitors, and so on.

Prospect file. This contains the same kinds of available information as customer files but is kept separate until a sale is made. After the sale, the card is transferred to the customer file.

Tickler file. This file is simply an elaborate calendar. The 3 × 5 cards are arranged by month and day to cover an entire year. The cards for the coming three months are broken down into individual days, whereas more distant months are not as detailed yet. As time goes by, upcoming months are broken down into individual days so that specific notes can be made on each day-card.

The tickler file helps you plan your time and keep track of appointments. If you have to call on an account every other Thursday, you would write it in on the appropriate card in the file. In your planning time, you can pull the cards for the coming week and see what your commitments are.

You may want to use different colored index cards to distinguish between customers and prospects; "A," "B," and "C" accounts; and even market segments or geographical locations. Too many colors can become confusing; decide on the best system for you. The tickler file should be cross-referenced to the customer and prospect files so that you can go from one to the other quickly for pertinent information.

Sales and customer service reports. This is a daily or weekly form that lists all of your calls and details about them. You'll enter things such as the type of call (personal, phone, letter), class of account, results, time required, needed follow-up, and so on. At the same time you should enter relevant data in your customer or prospect files and any new appointments in your tickler file. The master sheet lets you determine at a glance how you spent your week, giving you the overall picture.

Expense reports. Keep a record of all your expenses on a daily basis. They should be keyed to the customer or customers you spent the money on. In addition, the classification of the account and type of expenditure should be noted. Expenses will include things like gas, tolls, hotel, taxis, and meals.

Summary reports. These are reports that you make out at the end of the month and at the end of a planning period. They summarize the following areas:

1. *Sales*—Volume in units and dollars, volume by customer and market segment, percent increase or decrease over previous period, percentage of sales to calls.

2. *Accounts*—Number of accounts contacted, number of new accounts, percentage sold, number of accounts lost, number of new prospects.

3. *Profit*—Gross profit by market segment, overall territory profit, profit margins, ROTI's.

4. *Selling Expenses*—Total expenses, expenses per call, expenses per geographic locale, expenses per account classification.

5. *Qualitative Ratings*—Your strong points for the period in question; your weak points, areas of improvement, information needed for more effective sales.

6. *Miscellaneous*—Types of promotion used and their effectiveness; number of phone calls made and their outcomes; sales aids used; number of customer complaints filed; total commissions; number of days and hours worked; and so on.

As you can see, there is plenty of room for expanding the summary file to suit your needs. Often your company will give you forms which they require on a periodic basis. If these suffice for all your data, then you are in luck. If not, make up your own forms and have them photocopied. The insight you gain will be well worth the effort required to keep these records.

Analysis of Records

Periodically you will sit down with your records, summarize them, and analyze what has happened while you were busy working. In this chapter we have given you the tools to determine your strengths and weaknesses from these records. You now need to determine the causes of any problems which may be evident. The analysis of your problems will allow you to head off trouble before it has a negative effect on sales or your reputation. Problems usually occur slowly, so your intervention at an early stage will occur only if you monitor your territory.

Correction of Problems

The type of correction required is usually suggested by analysis of the problem. In general, however, you can ask yourself some questions to try to pinpoint areas that need work. Some of those questions are

1. "What unnecessary activities am I undertaking?" Under close scrutiny, many activities appear to be pursued for enjoyment rather than productivity. Often salespeople will call on a "C" account simply because they are in the neighborhood. The fact that the time could be better spent elsewhere occurs to them only after the fact. Try to think of the things in your day that you can cut out without missing them.

2. "What am I doing that can be done by someone else?" If you are in a position to delegate tasks, do so whenever possible. It is important to be objective in your evaluation of whether the other person can do the job. We often operate under the assumption that only we can do a specific job, when, in fact, it could be done by someone else. This is especially important to keep in mind when you realize how much your time is actually worth compared to a co-worker's.

3. "What activities should I be engaged in that I'm not?" This includes things like promotional activities, PR, personal education, prospecting, planning, and time management. This is a good time to set up goals for those activities that you should be doing.

4. "Have I set the right priorities?" That is, do you spend your time where it is most cost-effective? Do you think in terms of your ROTI when planning business activities?

THE FIVE COMMANDMENTS
OF TERRITORY MANAGEMENT

1. Analyze your territory, products and services, market segments competition, accounts, trends.
2. Set objectives based on the potential of your territory's potential.
3. Plan a strategy for the territory in general and for your individual accounts.
4. Keep accurate records.
5. Analyze your records periodically and set new objectives based on this analysis.

The management of a territory can make or break a salesperson's success. It is as much a part of selling as the face-to-face sales process itself.

six

Prospecting:
The Sales Pipeline

The goal of every salesperson is to make sales. Unlike most other businesses, in sales the purchase represents merely the tip of the iceberg. What lies below the tip, or in this case, before it, is much research, preparation, and legwork. If you haven't done the advance work, you might as well be selling to a penguin with bad credit.

To conceptualize the need for preparation, imagine that you are in the plant business. You grow house plants and carry 12 varieties, each of which blooms in a different month of the year. So you have a different plant available each month of the year. Each of these plants, however, requires 12 months to grow from seedling to full bloom. In addition, each plant requires attention once a month. This attention includes feeding, watering, pruning, rotation, and psychological counseling. So you set up a schedule in which you plant the seeds a year in advance and then every month do what is required to continue or start the growth of each plant. The pay-off doesn't come until a year after you've started, but each month thereafter a new plant will be ready to sell. You're all set, unless you forget a step some month. You will discover your oversight many months down the line. By then, however, it's too late. In the plant business, you can't plant the seeds on the thirtieth of the month and expect to have a sale on the first.

The development of your business as a salesperson also requires investing in a future payoff. The time lag between planting your seeds and reaping the rewards varies. Each month, however, you must do what is necessary to ensure a future yield. The maintenance and growth of your business requires that you

1.   Continually replenish your source of prospective clients.
2.   Qualify prospects to determine their eligibility as clients.
3.   Study the needs of each prospect.
4.   Propose solutions to prospects' problems.

Developing the habit of engaging in these activities routinely will provide a smooth flow of income in the future. A failure to tackle these activities conscientiously will create a "sales slump." (This is not a reference to your posture at the end of a hard day.)

THE CAUSE AND AVOIDANCE OF SALES SLUMPS

A sales slump is almost always due to negligence. Throughout the years we have found that salespeople who "get lazy" or ignore the cyclical nature of sales eventually experience slumps. Slumps can be avoided by maintaining an effective pipeline.

The illustration demonstrates the steps necessary in creating an effective sales pipeline. Starting at the top of the pipeline, you have an almost infinite source of prospects. Through the process of qualification, you reduce the infinite source to a realistic number. This group then enters the pipeline to be "processed." You contact the prospects and study their needs to determine how your product or service can help them. After preparing an intelligent proposal, you suggest several alternatives to the prospective client and confirm the sale. You have then added yet another client to your pool.

The flow from the reservoir of prospects to the pool of clients will be constant as long as you earnestly maintain each phase of the pipeline. This will result in a continual flow of income to you and make slumps a thing of the past.

THE RAW MATERIAL FOR YOUR PIPELINE

Productivity—whether of a factory, a writer, or a salesperson—requires raw material. In the sales business, your raw material is

Sales Pipeline

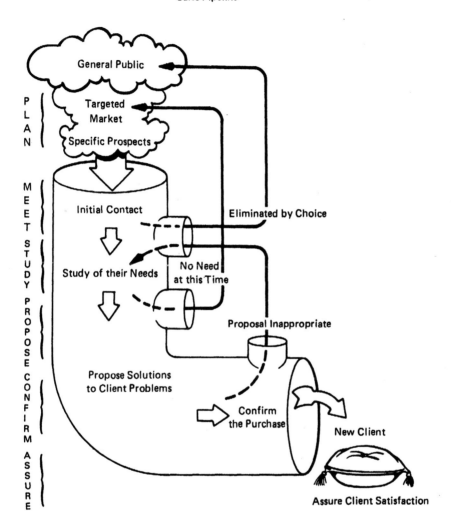

people. You, more than anyone else, must be a "people person." You want and need to meet new people constantly in order to maintain a steady flow through your sales pipeline.

As shown in the list that follows, the sources of prospects are quite extensive. They are so extensive, in fact, that many salespeople find them overwhelming. Having too many choices often makes decisions more difficult. As a salesperson, you need to be well-versed in all the proven methods of obtaining a prospect pool before choosing your best strategy. Only then can you professionally generate a virtually endless number of people to meet as prospects. The most accepted sources of prospects include the following:

1. Customers
2. Other prospects
3. Company leads
4. Friends and social contacts
5. Membership in civic and professional groups
6. Centers of influence
7. Canvassing
8. Conventions and trade shows
9. Directories, Yellow Pages
10. Tip clubs
11. Study groups
12. Direct mail
13. Newsletter
14. Seminars
15. Speaking
16. Personal observation

SOURCES OF PROSPECTS

Prospects can be found in all walks of life. For every person you meet there is a chance that he or she may need your product or service. Getting to these people is just a matter of time, technique, and perseverance.

Customers

Satisfied customers represent an excellent source of prospects for you. They'll talk to their friends and associates about their new purchase and they may mention your name. Occasionally a customer will tell you the name of an associate, but this is rare. So it's up to you to probe your customers tactfully for referrals. This is a habit you could cultivate after each sale or call. If you're always tactfully asking customers for referrals, perhaps they'll think of some for you even when you're not there. If nothing else, they'll be impressed with your enthusiasm and "stick-to-itivity."

Most professional salespeople say the most effective way to obtain referrals is to ask specific leading questions. One way of doing this is to review your list of qualifying criteria for prospects. Choose one criterion and base your question on it. For example, let's say one of your qualifying criteria is that the prospect has recently been promoted. You would then ask your client, "Who do you know who has recently been promoted?" You should then remain silent, giving your customer time to think. It's important to be quiet while clients think. If you keep on talking you'll only distract him and will end up with fewer names, if any.

If your first question doesn't produce any leads, run down your list of qualifying criteria and ask similar questions. Be sure to phrase the question so that it is *open-ended* rather than requiring a "yes" or "no" answer. The example above is an open-ended question. A close-ended question would be, "Do you know anyone who has recently been promoted?" It's too easy for a client just to say "No" if he can't think of anyone off-hand. An open-ended question, however, requires that he think for a moment.

When a customer is giving you referrals, especially if there's more than one, jot them down without analyzing them. After he's finished, you can go back and question him on qualifying details.

Your customers are some of the most valuable resources for referrals that you have. They know other business people in their field and are in the best position to recommend you to them. For this reason, you should ask your client if you can mention her name when contacting someone to whom she referred you. Through your customers you'll find new branches to follow to tap prospective clients.

Prospects

Prospects beget prospects. Many new salespeople assume that if a prospect doesn't buy, then there is no potential left in the relationship. Not so. A prospect can be asked for referrals in the same way that established clients are asked. With a prospect, however, it is paramount that you create a professional business relationship before asking for referrals. If you are perceived as being credible, trustworthy, and ethical your prospect will have no qualms about referring you to others. In fact, the better your relationship with a prospect, the harder he'll work to think of referrals for you. When they can, people like to help those they like.

Company Leads

Your company can furnish you with some very high-quality leads. They procure their leads from mailing programs, telephone solicitation, existing clients, and other sources. Sometimes your company will have also done the qualifying for you.

Company leads have the advantage of giving you credibility simply by virtue of being associated with your firm. Thus, you can immediately establish a trusting relationship and work on studying the prospect's problems. The prospects who come directly to your company often do so out of need. They may be shopping around for a particular product or service. The first salesperson to get to them can often make the sale if he or she handles it right. This is also true with competitive bidding. The first person to contact the prospect has the advantage. She can get information to which others might not have access. Being first, she will find the prospect still tolerant and willing to answer a lot of questions. In addition, the salesperson will be more impressive, showing enthusiasm by being first.

Friends and Social Contacts

Your family and friends can provide a rich source of prospects. It's not uncommon to learn that a salesperson's friends and relatives have only a vague idea of what he does. Now is the time to enlighten everyone as to the exact nature of your business. This should be a two-way communication. Not only will you tell them what you do, you'll also be sensitive to their needs. Whether you can sell to them is secondary. Like any prospect, they may be able to refer you to others. It's worthwhile to qualify your friends and relatives before contacting them. Let's say you're selling Lear Jets. Obviously, one qualifying criterion will be socioeconomic status. You would be wasting your time and embarrassing a friend or relative if you contacted them and *later* found out they're on welfare. It pays to do your homework. The following exercise, from Steve Curtis (of the Marketing Institute, Newport Beach, California), is designed to help you evaluate your opportunities among your friends. Please take the time now to fill out the "Friendship Tree."

Worksheet 6A
Friendship Tree

Friends that know your capabilities and degree of professionalism make a good "tree" for potential clients.

Demographic characteristics of each friend should be evaluated to maximize your time and to avoid waste their time. Age, occupation, length of time known, how well known, how often seen, ability to provide referrals, and how easy it is to approach this person are some factors to consider.

TYPE OF FRIEND   LIST TWO NAMES

School friends:

Friends of family:

Neighbors:

Known through spouse:

Known through children:

Known through hobbies:

Known through church:

Known through social clubs:

Known through community activities:

Known through past employment:

People you do business with:

Other:

In filling out the tree, you probably discovered opportunities that had previously escaped you. This will happen often as you become more and more aware of the innumerable sources of prospects that exist.

Once you've contacted your friends and relatives, devise a method of maintaining that contact on a regular basis. Start a mailing list and send them something periodically to keep them up to date on you. Newsletters, brochures, direct mail correspondence, and birthday cards will all serve you well.

It must be stressed, however, that when you approach a friend or relative, you do it in a low-keyed manner. Your sense of professionalism dictates that tact and sincerity are called for here. If you get the reputation of being overly aggressive, people will avoid you. Go about it in a matter-of-fact way at first. If they're interested, then put them on the mailing list and keep them informed. You have to be able to achieve a balance between social and business interests; otherwise, you'll be left with only business.

Membership in Civic and Professional Organizations

As an individual, become involved with your family, friends, and different community groups. You'll lead a more fulfilled life if you're active and interested in the world around you. Out of all of this will naturally come new social and business relationships. If you join a club or organization with the intention of "milking it" for its business, you'll end up miserable in the end. People can sense when they're being used.

Let's assume that you're participating in a professional organization for the same benefits as everyone else. There's certainly nothing wrong with letting people know what you do and of your willingness to be of service to them. In the natural course of conversation we're always asked, "What do you do?" The fastest way to turn people off is to launch into "I'm glad you asked . . . this week we're having a half-price special on one-legged panty hose, may I interest you in a pair?" It's to your advantage simply to tell them what you do and leave it at that. Later, if you see that you may be of some service to them, you can approach them and discuss it in a relaxed and helpful way. You don't have to "land" every prospect as he or she appears.

Once you get to know everyone in the organization (if it's small enough for you to do so), you can try to obtain a membership list or directory. You are then in a position to systematically contact each one—again in an informative, casual way. It's not advisable to send "blanket" direct mailings, unless you want to be the subject of organizational gossip. If people ask for brochures or information, by all means accommodate them. The idea is to enjoy the organization and the people in it. If you also broaden your prospect reservoir, then you've really lucked out. Chances are you will. The organizations you choose to join and participate in should be loaded with prospects within your priority target markets.

Centers of Influence

A center of influence is someone in a position to steer you to prospects or prospects to you. He or she is someone important to you for one reason or another. There are centers of influence in every facet of life and business. Centers of influence are also called opinion leaders. In order to ask a favor of someone who is going to influence the opinions of others, you must build rapport with the influential person. Opinion leaders as "contacts" are extremely valuable in any endeavor.

You'll find the following suggestions useful in dealing with centers of influence:

1. Focus on building a trusting relationship (rapport).
2. Be sure that they know the benefits you have given other clients.
3. Let them know your goals so they can be aware of the kind of prospects you're looking for.
4. Make sure they know that you sincerely want their help.
5. Give them a formal presentation describing your services or products.
6. Provide them with an extensive list of testimonials, personal and business references, and a professional resume. Centers of influence are very concerned about referring only those salespeople who will not undermine their reputations.

7. Be sure you report back to the center of influence after you contact the person referred.

8. Find some professional way to reciprocate or to say "thank you" (through your profession).

9. Get to know your center of influence. She might be a prospect herself without even realizing it.

Canvassing

I once heard a story about a very determined salesman. He was working in an amusement park, canvassing everyone, even 18-year-old kids. "Hi, I'm with the Dreamland Funeral Parlor . . . We're having a special this week on balsa wood coffins . . . I know you're a little young, but . . . " (the kids walked away, and he stood there wiping the two scoops of vanilla ice cream off his face, wishing they were chocolate, calling after them. . .) "We'll even throw in a custom stereo system!" Some people will do *anything* for a sale!

Most people think of sales in terms of a salesperson coming to the house, "getting his foot in the door," and "giving his pitch," even to deaf ears. Canvassing is the most criticized form of generating prospects, probably because it puts the prospect on the spot/in an uncomfortable position.

As a professional salesperson, you should be extremely selective in calling on people at random. Unsolicited calls, when little or no "homework" has been done on the prospect, are a low payoff, high-anxiety undertaking. Canvassing can be a potential source of prospects if you follow the steps outlined in the pipeline.

Before you contact people or firms in your area, they should be qualified. Because they are unsolicited prospects, study their situation to determine any obvious need for your service or product. You can then approach them in an intelligent fashion. Doing your homework will make you a credible salesperson from the beginning. This alone opens more doors than simply having a strong foot. If done with sincerity, interest, and research, canvassing can expand your prospect reservoir significantly.

Conventions and Trade Shows

Conventions and trade shows are to a salesperson like a candy store to a child. They are gold mines for prospecting. Attend as many trade shows and conventions as practical. Whether you are sent by your company or go on your own, you'll be going to accomplish the same goals for yourself:

1. Increase your knowledge of your industry.
2. Appraise the quality and type of convention or show. Analyze the show for possible individual or company participation in the future.
3. Determine the level and type of executive attendance there.
4. Impress delegates with yourself and your product or service.
5. Obtain as many prospects as possible.

Conventions are planned far in advance, often years. Do your homework before a convention or show. Find out who is attending or being represented. See if any of your company's present clients or prospects are planning to be there. Arrange to meet with them to solidify your business relationships.

At the convention, try to meet as many people as possible. Determine why they are there and what they think of the convention and its various workshops. Discuss the latest developments in your field. Ask them about their companies and try to uncover their needs. Also attend as many workshops and seminars as possible. Be sure to take notes and save all handouts, programs, brochures, and literature.

After the convention, follow up on your leads and prospects. Be sure to refresh their memories as to where and how you met. Often they will have pleasant recollections of the time you spent together at the convention.

When attending trade shows and conventions, save all your receipts because they are often tax deductible!

Directories

In addition to the Yellow Pages, your local library has directories on everything imaginable. Whether you're scouting out prospects in a particular area or creating a mailing list, directories will save you time and energy. Some directories list specific people to contact, such as corporate officers or department heads. Polk* publishes a directory that lists everyone living in every city in the United States. In some situations this can be very useful: Let's say you're selling dish antennas for satellite TV receivers. One of the things you'll want to know is who in your area can afford one. Consult the Polk Directory and look people up by their street address. Beside each address is the name and *occupation* of each resident. You are now in a position to send an introductory letter to as many people as you wish. The directory has given you their name, address, occupation, telephone number, and zip code. What more could you ask for?

You could ask for someone else to make the initial contact to determine if prospects are even remotely interested. Many companies accomplish this by having a telemarketing team. These people call, ask certain questions, and set appointments if the prospect is interested. This saves everyone time and money.

Tip Clubs

Many salespeople around the country have joined together to form small "tip clubs." The purpose of these groups is to make each member aware of the resources available from the other members. This type of give-and-take results in a group synergism—the branches of each person's prospecting tree are extended further outward. Each person is able to bring to the group his or her area of expertise, centers of influence, social networks, and business contacts. With everyone bouncing ideas off one another, a kind of professional kinetic energy develops in which everyone can gain information, cross-sell, obtain referrals, and increase the drive to achieve.

Most such groups meet on a regular basis over breakfast or lunch. They often have a short program during which a member can describe his or her product or service. Most "tip clubs" follow a few helpful guidelines:

---

*Check your library for the Polk Directory for your area.

1. *Establish a set of bylaws.* These can cover everything from the cost of lunch to ethical considerations of group interactions. An example of the latter might be that you don't use a member's name as a reference without having obtained permission.

2. *All expenses should be distributed evenly.* The fact that one member is a lawyer and another a telephone solicitor is irrelevant. The cost of meals, meeting rooms, speakers, and materials should be divided among the group on an equal basis.

3. *Shift the burden of running the group.* Periodically, the group should seek new volunteers to do whatever planning and arranging is necessary for the continuance of the meetings. This should be done in smaller increments than a year so that no one is unduly taxed with these chores.

4. *Limit membership to one representative in each field.* This will ensure that a cross-section of the community's resources are present while keeping the number of members manageable. The group could strive to have an accountant, sales reps in different fields, a lawyer, a banker, a public speaker, a writer, and so on.

Study Groups

Study groups have become a very effective tool for strengthening a salesperson in his or her career. A study group is an assemblage of individuals involved in *similar* yet not identical activities. They form close, business-related friendships in order to help each other grow and develop as sales professionals. At each meeting, they bring one another up to date by comparing notes on recent events, types of strategies planned, obstacles encountered and overcome, and other insights. Each member tries to strengthen the other members by offering observations, assessments, feedback, and support. Study groups become very creative, supportive environments in which each person can draw on the expertise and objectivity of others. A study group should always be kept noncompetitive. If the members are going after the same prospects, it is less likely that they will be open and supportive of one another. A study group could be viewed as your own personal board of directors.

Direct Mail

Direct mail as a means of prospecting offers the major advantage of allowing you to reach a large number of people without being physically present. There are two basic kinds of direct mail strategies—one-time mailings and "campaigns." The one-time mailing is aimed at generating an immediate response to an attractive offer. The "campaign" or "conditioning" method seeks to make the prospect increasingly more aware of you as a viable answer to her needs in a particular area. This involves a long-term campaign to create confidence and interest in your abilities as a professional salesperson. Many experts believe, as do we, that direct mailings should be followed by personal phone calls, within two to four weeks after the mailing. Although this is time-consuming, it can significantly increase your "hit" ratio.

Mailing lists.   No matter how effective your direct mail letter, if you send it to the wrong prospects you've wasted your time and money. *Who* you mail to is more important than what you mail to them. *What* you send however, cannot be thought of as anything *less* then secondary.

Where will you get your mailing lists? In every major city there are firms that do nothing but compile mailing lists. You can rent these lists for $25.00 or more per thousand names. Renting a list from a list broker offers many advantages:

1. *Categorized lists.* A list broker has already taken the time to classify his lists by many different variables. Some of these include geographic location, yearly income, demographics, age, interests, and so on. The larger the broker, the greater your choices will be. You may be able to save time in qualifying your prospects by asking for a specific type of list.

2. *Business expense.* Renting a mailing list is a business expense and therefore often tax deductible.

3. *Zip-code ordered.* When you're sending out a mailing to more than 200 addressees you can take advantage of bulk mailing rates. This requires separating the mail into groups by zip code. A rented list is already categorized by zip code, saving you hours of work. Bulk mail permits must be

obtained from the post office but are worth the nominal fee.

4. *Computer-ready.* The mailing list you get from a broker is available in a form which makes it ready to feed into a computer. You can then employ a typing service with word processors to print out the address labels automatically.

5. *Clean and up-dated.* Most list brokers will guarantee that the list is current and has no "dirty" addresses on it. Dirty addresses are those which cause the letter to come back marked "addressee unknown" or "return to sender."

Directories (again). Depending upon the size of your mailing, you may want to compile your own mailing list. This can easily be done by using the same directories we discussed as sources of prospects. In fact, whether you rent a list or not, you may want to go through local directories and add companies which may not be on your rented list.

Personal mailing list. As a professional salesperson you should develop your own file of people to whom you'll send mailings. This file can be accumulated over time and, like any list, needs to be cleaned periodically. Whenever you meet a prospect, trade business cards with him. Don't immediately throw that card into your mailing list, however, because he may not qualify. So qualify all new prospects for your personal mailing list just as you would if you planned to call on them in person.

When compiling your mailing list, it pays to be organized! Have separate lists with categories such as:

- Customers already doing business with the company
- High-potential prospects
- Low- to medium-potential prospects
- Centers of influence
- Friends, relatives, and miscellaneous

You then need to determine when each of these groups should be contacted and how often. For example, you may want to contact pre-existing customers on a quarterly basis and low-potential prospects once a year. Mark your calendar and devise other systems for organization. It pays off in the long run.

Typically, direct mail yields a low percentage return. One to three percent is often good when you figure in the cost of developing the letter, postage, mailing lists, and so on. The sales on just one to three percent can be quite sizable. Be sure to measure the cost by average sale expected. You want people to be reminded of you and your ability to be of service to them in some way.

Direct Mail Techniques

What you send is second in importance only to whom you send it to. When your prospect opens your mailing you want him to read it and to be interested in finding out more about you and your services. To increase the chances of this happening, you must design the mailing so that it will be attractive, easy-to-read, and informative. See page 157 for an example.

Direct mail has become a science; for the most part, experts agree on how it should be done (a feat in itself!). In general, the mailing should observe the following rules:

1. *Make it personal.* A letterhead should appear at the top of the page so the prospect can identify the mailer immediately. This may stop her from throwing it in the trash. If your prospect is interested, your letterhead will prevent her from having to search the page for your name and address.

2. *Cover only one idea.* It's often tempting to cram in as much information as will fit on the page. The rationale behind this is, "As long as I'm going through the time and expense, I might as well get as much exposure as I can." This is not a sound advertising practice. You must keep the mailing as simple and straightforward as possible. Be satisfied covering one idea well. As you will see, you won't have the room for more than one concept if you develop your mailing correctly. So aim for simple effectiveness (rather than complex chaos).

3. *Focus on benefits, not features.* This means you should stress *what* effect you want. How the effect is achieved is important to you. That is, think of yourself as a consumer. If you're considering buying a food processor, you're more

Cathcart
INSTITUTE
Business Growth Specialists

Name and Address

Dear _____(first name)__:

You can increase sales and decrease the need for supervision.

In just fifteen minutes a day your sales force can become self-starters and sharpen their sales skills. My newest professional training series, The Eight Competencies of Sales Leadership is the millenium version of my original program Relationship Selling. I've rewritten it including fifteen years of new research and recorded it into over 160 separate five-minute sales "skill sessions."

This program is specifically designed to increase the amount of initiative and self-leadership among sales professionals. It improves all eight of the primary competencies required to become a sales leader.

To sample the value of this program for you, please fax or mail back this letter with your note "send me a sample" written below, or email me at   .
Either way, we will assure that you receive a CD with a representative sample of the power and value of this sales library.

For more information on Cathcart Institute, Inc. simply visit
on the web and let us know how you would like to advance your sales results this year.

In The Spirit of Growth,
Jim Cathcart
CEO, Founder
Cathcart Institute, Inc.

__ Yes, Send me a sample.
_____(Your signature)_____
Date: _____

PO Box 9075
La Jolla, CA 92038
(858) 456-3813 • (800) 222-4883

fax: (858) 456-7218
e-mail: Info@Cathcart.com
website: www.cathcart.com

1988-89 *President of the National Speakers Association* • *Member of Speakers Roundtable*

interested in all the things it can do than how or why it does them. That's the engineer's concern.

4. *Make it easy to read and attractive.* If you pick up a mailing that looks like a solid page of a book, chances are you won't read it. Let's face it, everyone is lazy. Your mailing must look attractive and draw your prospect in. For this reason it should not look like solid text. This effect can be achieved by staggering the left-hand paragraph margin every couple of paragraphs. Use colors to emphasize different sections and important points. Arrange the page so that it looks interesting.

Development of Effective Mailing

Mailings should have a logical flow. They should aim to answer the reader's unconscious questions as they arise.

- "What is it?"
- "What does it do?"
- "How would *I* use it?"
- "Oh yeah, prove it!" or "Interesting, but I'd like a second opinion."
- "If I'm interested, how do I get one?"
- "How much does it cost?"

Your mailing should answer these questions in a way that impresses your prospects. The best way to impress is to adhere to the following five steps.

Description.   Describe the product or service in a concise, attractive way, without claiming miracles. Be sincere and let the facts speak for themselves. For example, you might say "We have a training program available which will make your salespeople much more aware of the number of prospects they can contact."

Illustration.   Examples speak louder than descriptions. In this case, you might show a copy of a letter of appreciation from a former client. (Naturally the letter would have to be photo-reduced.)

Dear Cathcart, Alessandra and Associates: It is my pleasure to report to you that your Seminar on Prospecting was a complete success! Within a month, every member of our sales team had increased his prospect file by 25 percent and sales have increased an average of 14 percent. People are still talking about how effective your methods are once they adapted them to their target markets . . . etc.

The point will be made.

Claim on your behalf. You are then in a position to promise the same results for your prospect. "Your company can see the same increase in sales and prospects after our three-hour seminar!"

Proof. This is the time to soothe the skeptical beast that afflicts most prospects. Your prospect may be thinking, "OK, that's *one* company that it worked for. Big deal . . ." You can now dispense with humility and show them how good you are. You may want to quote magazine articles or other reviews, as if advertising a movie.

"*By far the most valuable seminar we've ever sponsored.*" Kirk Steeltoe, Mgr., Midwest Marketing Enterprises.

"*. . . makes prospecting something tangible for a change.*" Rocko Green, Chairman, Multi-National Multi-Level Marketing, Inc.

Call for action. Now that your prospect is interested (think positive!), you need to use words which will spur him on to action. Using action words will help motivate. "Call our toll-free number now to find out more about how your sales team can gain the competitive edge!" Or you might encourage prospects to act by offering a special deal. "Increase your sales prospects! Send the enclosed postcard by November 30 and get 10 percent off our three-hour seminar!" Both of these examples achieve three things. They repeat the claim, make it easy to respond, and use action words. To increase the ease of response in the second example, you would be sure to enclose a self-addressed stamped postcard.

After you've designed and laid out your mailing, double-check it for mistakes. You should also show it to someone who can react to it objectively. Often we are too emotionally wrapped up in our creations to see the mistakes in them.

Follow-up

Needless to say, you'll follow up any responses to your mailing. Go one step further. Choose those companies you wish you had heard from and follow up on them whether they respond or not. It's very possible that the combination of the mailing and a personal contact will prove advantageous.

RECORD KEEPING

This section will show you how a dull pain now can prevent a migraine later. Keeping records allows you to know what you're accomplishing and to do more of it in the future if it's producing results. If you know your gross profit and expenses for any given mailing, you can determine your R.O.I. and W.I.W.M.T.M. Your R.O.I. is the Return on your Investment. Did you make 5 percent, 10 percent, or 50 percent? If your R.O.I. was low, could you have improved the mailing in some way? Would the money have earned you more interest in the bank? If so, you should figure out why your R.O.I. was so low. Once you know whether you made any money, you'll know your W.I.W.M.T.M.—Was It Worth My Time and Money? Hopefully it was, but you'll know only if you keep careful records.

Another reason to keep good records is for tax purposes. Every penny you spend on a mailing is an expenditure for business and is probably deductible at tax time. Your accountant or tax preparer may need to see your records and the IRS certainly will if you are audited. Your records will save you money in the long run.

To take the guesswork out of cost analyses and to help you be more organized, we've included a worksheet (6-B) for keeping track of your direct mail costs. The mail campaign budget breaks down your expenses from the development of the mailing to the sale of merchandise. It will give you a total of all your expenses to deduct from your gross profit. Keeping accurate records is one of the many habits cultivated by professional salespeople.

Worksheet 6B
Direct Mail Campaign Budget for One Mailing

NAME OF MAIL PIECE: _____

OBJECTIVE: _____

DATE: _____

PREPARED BY: _____

A. DIRECT EXPENSES

1. Planning/Administrative/Operating
   Salaries (Man Hours x Hourly Rate) $ _____

2. Creative Costs/Preparations
   a. Copy $ _____
   b. Layout $ _____
   c. Artwork $ _____
   d. Photography/
      Retouching $ _____
   e. Printing
      Preparation $ _____

4. Other enclosure $ _____

5. Envelopes $ _____

6. Mailing list rental/purchase $ _____

7. Mailing list maintenance $ _____

8. Mailing piece preparation
   (folding, collating, inserting,
   labeling, addressing, metering,
   sorting, typing, etc.) $ _____

9. Postage
   a. Outgoing $ _____
   b. Return $ _____ $ _____

10. If Selling Merchandise
    a. Cost of merchandise $ _____
    b. Handling $ _____
    c. Postage/shipping $ _____
    d. Royalties $ _____
    e. Refunds/cancellations $ _____
    f. Refurbish returns $ _____
    g. Bad debts $ _____
    h. Storage $ _____ $ _____

11. Other $ _____

TOTAL DIRECT EXPENSES $ _____

NEWSLETTERS

The rate of technical advancement in practically every field is so great that few individuals can keep abreast of it. If you are selling in one of these fields and have a thorough understanding of the changes as well as a knack for writing, you're in a prime position to issue a newsletter. Let's use microcomputers as an example. The home and small business computer market changes almost daily as new models and options are introduced. As an enterprising salesperson, you could develop a newsletter in which you call attention to new products, services, and technological improvements. Mailing a monthly newsletter of this type would certainly be a service to your clients and prospects. They would appreciate your saving them time and would keep you in mind as someone with whom to do business. Page 163 contains an example of the authors' newsletter (front page).

The difficult part for you is finding the time to read, simplify, and rewrite newsworthy information. Keep in mind that a good newsletter should be

1. *Sent out regularly*. Remember that consistency and regularity prove how serious you are.
2. *Brief*. No advertising, fish stories, or poetry for filler. Just meat.
3. *Clear*. Your writing must be concise, informative, and directed to the people to whom you're sending it.
4. *Accurate*. Your credibility is at stake. Make sure your facts are accurate.
5. *Personal*. Write your newsletter as if you were the reader's personal consultant. Giving advice and your opinion is OK as long as you make it clear that it's *strictly* your opinion.

SEMINARS AND CLASSES

For the professional salesperson, appearing as a lecturer or teacher is an exciting and rewarding way to gain exposure. You can offer to teach evening classes at local colleges and adult education programs. Large corporations occasionally hold seminars to improve their employees' skills. These all provide prime opportunities for you to become regarded as an expert in your field.

You may see the need for a seminar in a particular area but feel you don't have the expertise or time to conduct it yourself. In this

THE

CATHCART/ALESSANDRA
REPORT

In This Issue:

- *IMPROVING YOURSELF*
- *3 NEW ASSOCIATES*
- *EXPANDED SERVICES*
- *BEHAVIORAL STRATEGIES*
- *SPEAKING SCHEDULES*

THE BIG MOVE OF CATHCART, ALESSANDRA & ASSOCIATES

It's final! Jim Cathcart and family have moved from Tulsa, Oklahoma to San Diego, California. His partner, Tony Alessandra, already resides in La Jolla.

Their company—Cathcart, Alessandra & Associates, Inc.—will now be positioned for even greater growth than when Jim and Tony lived 1,500 miles apart. Their ability to creatively develop and market new products will increase now that they will work in the same office. Jim expects to be fully operational in San Diego before the end of March 1983.

It was less than four years ago that Jim and Tony first met. In June 1979, both Jim and Tony were keynote speakers at a Century 21 Convention at the San Diego Hilton. The personal and philosophical chemistry between the two of them was very strong from the moment they met. Jim got Tony actively involved in the National Speakers Association and should be given much credit for the tremendous success Tony has had to date as a professional speaker. Tony, on the other hand, played a significant role in helping Jim develop and market books, films and audio cassette programs.

In early 1981, Jim and Tony decided to formally become partners. They formed an Oklahoma corporation called Cathcart, Alessandra & Associates, Inc. (Tony lost the coin toss!) Their corporate mission is to develop and effectively market an ever-improving line of top quality products and services designed to enhance business people's effectiveness in self-management, interpersonal communications, management and sales.

In less than two years since their incorporation, Tony and Jim have developed three sales books, a six-cassette audio tape program, a video cassette training module on handling objections, a four-cassette audio tape program on how to deal with the differences in people, and a twenty-eight video cassette training program on self-improvement. All these products were developed while Jim and Tony lived 1,500 miles apart. Now you can see why they are so excited about what they can accomplish and create once they are together full-time in sunny Southern California. *Wish us luck!*

This Newsletter is a new undertaking for Cathcart, Alessandra & Associates. It is our way of communicating four times per year with our past and present clients as well as our friends and colleagues. Each issue will contain current information about Jim and Tony as well as their speaking schedule in case anyone would like to preview them. Each issue will also contain a timely article that any organization can reprint by simply asking written permission from us. Also included will be information about new products and services developed by Jim and Tony.

We strongly encourage any of our readers to give us feedback on this Newsletter so that we can make it a worthwhile reading experience for everyone who receives it. Any interesting news clippings, training trends or intriguing stories are more than welcome from our readers. We will gladly give credit for any material that comes from our readers which we use in our Newsletter.

Fable for Trainers

Once upon a time, the animals decided they must do something heroic to meet the problems of "a new world." So they organized a school. They adopted an activity curriculum consisting of running, climbing, swimming and flying. To make it easier to administer the curriculum, *all* the animals took *all* the subjects.

The *duck* was excellent in swimming, but he made only passing grades in flying and was very poor in running so he had to stay after school and drop swimming in order to practice running.

The *rabbit* started at the top of the class in running, but had a nervous breakdown because of so much makeup work in swimming.

The *squirrel* was excellent in climbing until he developed frustration in the flying class. He got a C in climbing and a D in running.

At the end of the year, an abnormal *eel* could swim exceedingly well, and also run, climb and fly a little, had the higher average, and was the valedictorian.

—UKA

THE MORAL: For higher productivity, focus on the strength of your people, not their weaknesses.

case, hire a speaker under your sponsorship. When you sponsor a speaker, let it be known that you're doing so. After the seminar, provide a question-and-answer period in which you participate. Also, hand out product brochures and promotional materials to ensure your exposure.

The most valuable time after a class or seminar is when you socialize, listen to participants' individual needs, and schedule future contacts. This is the primary reason you're there.

PUBLIC SPEAKING

Civic clubs, professional organizations, corporations, conventions, and church groups are constantly seeking effective speakers to address their groups. If you can develop your skills as a speaker, you'll find this avenue to be highly rewarding and fruitful as a prospect generation source.

The speech you give as a public speaker needs to be much more general than the one you give as a lecturer or teacher. Remember not to be commercial! Focus on the broad subject under which your area of expertise lies.

There are two effective ways to gain prospects from a public speaking engagement. You can distribute response cards on which interested prospects fill in their names and phone numbers. A more effective method is to hold a drawing. Bring along a gift or offer a discount on your firm's product. To enter the drawing, the participants simply drop a business card, preferably their own, into a box from which you will pick the winner. You'll then have scores of names to qualify later as prospects. You can also offer to send a free article on your speech topic to any attendees who give you their business cards. When you mail the article, you can also include information about yourself, your company, and your products/services.

PERSONAL OBSERVATION

Prospecting can take place whether you're wearing your three-piece suit or not. This is true, however, only when it becomes *second nature*. Once you have conditioned yourself to recognize a prospect in any situation, you can act on the insight with a mailing, personal contact, conversation, and so on. You'll find prospects in the newspaper, on TV talk shows, at parties, waiting in line, and in the doctor's office. The key is to have the qualifications firmly planted in your mind so that those types of people will "jump out at you."

By now you see that prospects are ubiquitous—they are everywhere! Ways of contacting them are also so numerous that they can be overwhelming. It is important for you to analyze your current sales situation and determine the sources that will be most productive for you. This will help you maximize your use of time. The Prospecting Action Plan (Worksheet 6C) will clarify your prospecting goals and suggest action steps in achieving these goals. Take the time now to choose five sources (of the several we have described in this chapter) from which you would like to generate prospects. Think carefully about this. The five should be the ones which will yield the greatest number of *qualified* prospects. Under each of the five sources list the strategies to be used.

QUALIFY YOUR PROSPECTS

The failure to qualify a prospect will cause you considerable frustration and loss of time and money; it will decrease your efficiency. Remember that a prospect is only someone who has a need for your product or service. A *qualified* prospect not only has the need, but also the means to act. Your call-to-sale (closing) ratio will be much higher if you qualify each prospect before making your call. Qualifying a prospect involves three basic steps:

1. Set the conditions for qualifying your prospects. Make a checklist of important prospect characteristics such as position in company, credit, and so on.
2. Determine whether your prospect possesses these factors.
3. Decide whether this is a good time to initiate contact with this prospect. Timing is often essential.

If you're scientific about your prospecting, you'll increase your prospect reservoir and know exactly how you did it. This makes for future success rather than a "hit or miss" career. Adopt these systems for yourself:

- *Avoid confusion.* Be organized! Keep a good file system. If necessary, get help in setting it up. When prospects are filed, make a log entry detailing where the prospect came from— referral, directory, cold contact, etc.

Worksheet 6C
Prospecting Action Plan

DIRECTIONS: Write out techniques to increase your exposure and generate more prospects from these sources:

Source _____
1.   A. _____

   B. _____

   C. _____

   D. _____

Source _____
2.   A. _____

   B. _____

   C. _____

   D. _____

Source _____
3.   A. _____

   B. _____

   C. _____

   D. _____

Source _____
4.   A. _____

   B. _____

   C. _____

   D. _____

Source _____
5.   A. _____

   B. _____

   C. _____

   D. _____

- *Monitor your results.* One of the great dangers in prospecting is the tendency to ease off as soon as the reservoir has swelled. Names alone are not enough, prospects must be qualified and moved into the pipeline for contacting.

- *Try different techniques.* Analyze and evaluate your prospecting system and your R.O.I. Discover which sources pay off best for you.

- *Follow up.* Imagine what not following through would do to your golf game. The effect is worse in sales. Having a file full of prospects' names makes you "prospect rich" but doesn't increase your income.

There are literally acres and acres of diamonds (prospects) sitting out there waiting to be picked up. If you can cultivate an awareness of the sources and the discipline to pursue them, you'll never have a sales slump and you'll be handsomely rewarded for your efforts. This is what sales is all about.

seven

Promotional Strategies

In the sales profession, there are two ways of getting business. You can *go out* after it or it can *come to you.* The former is accomplished by prospecting, as we discussed in the last chapter. Having business come to you is the primary objective of promotional strategies.

We would all agree that it's much more pleasant and less time consuming having prospects come to you. "Warm prospects" make life easier by

1. Being better qualified.
2. Being ready to buy (timing!).
3. Knowing more specifically what their buying needs are.
4. Having decided that you and your product or services are worth their time to investigate.
5. Being less price-sensitive than "cold" prospects. It's also very flattering when prospects knock on *your* door looking to do business with *you!*

Promotional strategies are techniques which give you positive exposure to your target market. Your prospects will know who you are, whom you represent and what products or service you have to offer. This will smooth the way for setting up an appointment.

If your prospect has been made aware of you in advance, you will find it much easier to establish the relationship, set up an appointment, and eventually consummate the sale. Promotion will give you, your company, and your product the *name recognition* you need.

In the selling business, timing is crucial. Contacting prospects puts the control in your hands. You choose when to call on them. There is always the chance, however, that they will not be ready to buy. In this case, you make a note as to when to contact them again in the future. Hopefully, your timing will be better.

The beauty of promotional strategies is that they plant a seed in your prospect's mind. In effect, you've made a "reservation" to be considered for future business. When you're in the back of the prospect's mind, the chances are good that you'll be called when he or she is in the market for your product or service. This doesn't guarantee you'll get the sale, but at least you'll be able to compete for it. Prospecting doesn't necessarily create a lasting impression. So if your timing is off, you may never get another chance. Promotional strategies increase your future chances significantly. The knowledge you gain from this chapter will help you encourage business to come to you.

PROMOTIONAL STRATEGY

The professional salesperson will always be involved in promotion to augment and improve the effectiveness of day-to-day calls. A properly executed promotional program will aim to accomplish the following objectives:

1. Introduce your service or product to new prospects and smooth the way for setting appointments.
2. Encourage more purchases by current clients.
3. Encourage off-season purchases.
4. Compete with competitors' promotional efforts and keep present customers.
5. Enlarge your market by encouraging activity in a wider geographic area.
6. Contact former customers with reminders of your services.

Ultimately all promotion is directed at increasing sales. Some strategies, such as advertising and sales promotion, are designed to do this directly. They are often bold, explicit forms of gaining the prospect's favor. Publicity and public relations, on the other hand, influence sales indirectly by encouraging the buyer to think highly of you and your company. Most people would rather buy from a person or company they "like," even if they don't know them personally.

Salespeople usually think of promotional programs as being in the domain of their companies. Corporations have the resources available to develop and execute comprehensive promotional programs. As a professional salesperson, however, you should think in terms of being your own company. Promotion is as important to you as it is to a large corporation, but on a smaller scale. Become familiar with all your promotional options in order to select those which will be most effective for you. The principal types of promotional strategies at your disposal are

Advertising
- Ads in the Yellow Pages
- Ads in trade magazines and newspapers
- Direct mail
- Brochures and flyers
- TV
- Radio

Sales promotion
- Sales aids such as pens, calendars, novelties
- Special events/open houses
- Exhibits at trade shows and conventions
- Discounts for off-season or special purchases (coupons, package deals)
- In-store demonstrations

Public relations and/or publicity
- Christmas, birthday, special-occasion cards
- Membership in professional associations and clubs
- Donations of time or money

- Speaking engagements, seminars
- Press releases, interviews

In some fields, promotion is more important than the product being sold. Without promotion of some type, it is difficult to sell anything. Effective promotion, however, makes it possible to sell practically *anything!* The "pet rocks" which sold so well a few years ago are a case in point.

ADVERTISING

Advertising is a paid, persuasive presentation which promotes you, your company, and your product or service. Advertising has become more and more sophisticated in its attempts to influence the buying behavior of its target markets. No matter how subtle or obvious the ad is, the desired outcome can be achieved only through:

Education—Making prospects aware of yourself or your product, either for the first time or as a reminder.

Preference formation—After making prospects aware of your existence, you must form an attitude in their minds. You and your product must be liked. When there is competition, however, you must be *more* than liked. You must be *preferred.* You have to create the advantage that will cause your prospects to choose you over "them."

Affecting the purchase decision—You can educate your prospects and be so preferred that you will be remembered in their wills! If you don't get their business, however, your advertising hasn't been effective. Your R.O.I. will be high only if you convince prospects that you are the best game in town and they must own you (your product, that is).

Repeat business—Imagine how much more difficult your job would be if you sold to each client only once! You would need an infinite number of markets and prospects. Repeat business, especially when *they* come to *you,* is what makes the extra effort in sales worthwhile. An ongoing promotional program will strengthen and solidify your clients' preference for you.

Now that you know the objectives of the game, determine which league you want to be in. The size of your business and the nature of your target market will determine which advertising means you will use. If you're a sales consultant and public speaker, it obviously won't pay for you to advertise on TV or with fliers. A more effective medium would be trade journals. See Page 174 for a full-page ad by two professional speakers in a trade journal.

In determining which sources would best fill your needs, you should ask yourself several questions:

1. What message do I want to convey? Should more emphasis be put on me or my product? With what themes am I going to try to associate myself and my product ?

2. Who am I trying to reach? Who is my target audience?

3. Where will they be most likely to see my message? Should I buy a billboard in a subway car to advertise my karate classes?

4. How much can I afford to spend on advertising this year? Can I afford *not* to spend money on advertising? (Only you can determine this. There is no hard and fast rule for the percentage of gross sales which should be spent on advertising.)

5. When is the best time to schedule my advertising? (Did you ever notice how income tax services advertise less during the summer or fall? There's a good reason for this.)

After thoroughly exploring these basic questions, you can then take your choice of the following available sources:

TV	Newspapers	Novelties
Radio	Direct Mail	Handbills/Fliers
Magazines	Billboards	Displays

Some of these are better suited for companies than for individuals, and vice-versa. Over time, patterns have emerged which indicate that some sources are better for salespeople than others. Ranked in order of the highest to lowest value, the most proven promotions or methods in the selling business are:

CATHCART, &ALESSANDRA associates, inc.

A CONSULTING FIRM SPECIALIZING IN "HELPING PEOPLE GROW"

CUSTOM-DESIGNED TRAINING PROGRAMS

Seminars and Workshops

For a lasting improvement in behavior to take place, the participants must become INVOLVED in the learning process. Our indepth workshops carefully lead your people through the logic of concept and then actively include them in the experience of learning. Sales, Human Relations, Effective Listening, Self Management and other topics are taught in an entertaining and playful style which makes it **fun to learn.** The focus is on learning, yet the format is lively and enjoyable. Available in half day, full day or longer formats.

JIM CATHCART, C.S.P.

Jim Cathcart conducts over 100 programs each year in locations ranging from Bermuda to the Bering Sea. As an author and film personality, he has developed numerous books, articles and recorded programs.

He currently serves on the Board of Directors of the National Speakers Association Jim's experiences include Planner for 5 major international conventions, Training Director for a large corporation and management consultant to organizations worldwide. A man of many talents, but most of all a man who cares about Helping People Grow.

Professional Speakers*

Tony and Jim collectively give over 200 presentations each year across the continent. Whether your need is for a banquet keynote or a Sales Campaign kickoff, you'll get a high-impact presentation every time. **(Send for a sample recording today.)**

Strategic Planning Sessions

To truly get the most from an annual strategic planning session, it is best to utilize an outside facilitator to lead the discussion. We are widely experienced in turning otherwise dull meetings into exciting, creative experiences **grounded in practical application** that produce specific action plans for achieving your goals

CATHCART, ALESSANDRA
& ASSOCIATES, INC.
P.O. Box 2767
LA JOLLA, CALIFORNIA
92038

Jim —
"Since we began using Jim's services in 1976 our agency has grown from $17 million in annual sales,to over $100 million! You can bet that we will continue to turn to Jim Cathcart to help us grow."
Joe Willard
General Agent
Massachusetts Mutual Life Insurance

Tony —
"Another super job by a super pro. I was fortunate enough to hear part of your presentation and I must say you had your audience spellbound. Our audience is a pretty astute group who hear the best speakers in the country and they rank you up there with the best. You had the largest sign-up of any session on the program."
Bob Radke
Manager of Education
Meeting Planners International

Business and Personal Consultation

Successful executives and top sales people regularly call on us to provide consultation to meet specific needs Subjects covered vary from Self Development to Time Control, Sales Development, Marketing Planning, Goal Setting, Platform Skills and Family Communications.

With Jim and Tony you'll discover that a professional speaker is not an expense, but an investment in the greater productivity of your people.

*As evidence of their expertise on the platform, both Jim and Tony have earned the designation Certified Speaking Professional (CSP) from the prestigious National Speakers Association

TONY ALESSANDRA, Ph.D.

Dr. Anthony J. Alessandra is a nationally noted professional speaker who has the unique ability to educate an audience with practical information in a way that it is put to immediate use in their personal and professional lives. Averaging over 100 paid speeches each year, his messages are well-seasoned with humor and quite motivating

A prolific writer, Tony is the author of many articles and books including **Non-Manipulative Selling** and **The Art of Managing People.** Besides playing a leading role in the top-selling film, "The Power of Listening," Tony is under contract with Walt Disney Productions to develop a series of sales training films based on his book

1. Person-to-person	Higher Value
2. Telephone	↑
3. Mail or personal letter	
4. Form letter	
5. General promotional mailing	↓
6. Trade journal, newsletter, or publication	Lower Value

As can be seen by their relative strengths, one good combination is a personal letter of introduction prior to personal contact.

Billions of dollars are spent each year on advertising in this country. Its effectiveness is undeniable. For example, in 1947, Volkswagen was an unknown car manufacturer. In the early 1970's, Volkswagen was the largest selling imported car in the United States! Advertising works!

SALES PROMOTION

Sales promotions include activities other than personal selling and advertising, which directly affect sales. Sales promotions differ from overall promotion in that they relate to one-time activities. Overall promotion is the marketing program or "umbrella" which includes sales promotions, advertising, and so on. Sales promotions involve gimmicks, special sales, demonstrations, and other business stimulators that are temporary in nature.

Some of the more common sales promotions are

1. Demonstrations of new products—either live or on audio-video displays.
2. Exhibit booths at trade shows or conventions.
3. Promotional packages, special "year-end" sales and other discounts.
4. Free calendars, matches, pens, and other novelties to be remembered by.
5. Christmas cards.
6. Attractions such as celebrities, raffles, etc.
7. Discount coupons.

As an individual salesperson, you should think up new ways to promote sales, especially if your company does not. Keeping an eye on the calendar and knowing when a product needs to be sold most heavily will allow you to plan ahead. Begin your sales promotion early so that the awareness has been established when the season arrives. You've probably noticed that the clothing and fashion industry begins advertising months ahead of time. Buyers in the clothing business plan their inventories at least one season in advance. Again, timing is important.

If your company is already involved with sales promotions, decide how you can take advantage of them. If the company is setting up a booth at a trade show or convention, volunteer to work the booth. This is a valuable place to prospect. At the show, give out your business card and get one from everyone with whom you talk business. Try to set appointments while you're still at the show rather than calling everyone after the show.

If your company gives out calendars every year, you can stamp your name and phone number on the calendar. You can also have other items made up with your name, company, and phone number on them. Just make sure that whatever sales promotion item you use carries your personal and company image. It must be consistent.

Whether you're an independent or a representative of a large company, you can always come up with sales promotion ideas. Not only do they create an immediate sales impact, but many sales promotional items have a long life and can remind your clients and prospects about you, your company, and your product throughout the year.

PUBLIC RELATIONS

Public relations means relating to the public in a way which wins their appreciation. It involves good will, altruism, and community awareness. Its effect on sales is indirect and therefore more difficult to analyze. Sales do improve, however, because people like to do business with firms that take a interest in the community. In determining your best public relations strategies, you should analyze several questions:

Who are your "publics?" "Publics" are groups of people who perceive you as a business person. Some of these publics act on their perceptions to increase your sales. Others just appreciate you. It is important for you to identify each of your publics and to develop strategies for improving your image in their eyes. For example, if you are selling real estate, your publics would be bankers, mortgage companies, customers, the community at large, other brokers, property managers, and so on.

What methods are available to reach these publics? There are many avenues open to you. Your choices will be determined by your personal interests and finances. Your company may engage in a wider range of PR activities simply because it can afford to. Then again, some companies do virtually nothing for PR. For example, a defense industry selling exclusively to the government doesn't need to be concerned about public image, advertising, or sales promotion.

Public relations comes in many forms. Like advertising methods, some of these will be viable for you and some won't.

Community activities are geared toward helping the community. These usually involve social functions including benefits for under-privileged children, campaigns for commuity awareness and pride, contributions to a community event such as a carnival, and so on.

Contributions of time or money to all kinds of groups. This includes sponsoring Little League teams, sporting events, cultural activities, charities, community development programs, and other worthy causes.

Public speeches. You, as an individual salesperson, can offer your service, free of charge, to a group who would like to hear you speak on your area of expertise. Large corporations also make speakers available as a public service.

Public services. Many TV and radio stations sponsor information services such as ski reports, surf reports, entertainment guides, medical tips, traffic reports, and other community services.

Staged events. Companies may sponsor picnics, anniversary parties, softball games, or other events. Your presence at these events gives members of the organization a chance to get to know you and feel comfortable with you in a relaxed setting.

Trade associations. Belonging to trade associations and interest groups provides good PR for individuals and companies. Your membership shows that you care about the industry. You can also generate many prospects from your participation.

What is the image you want to convey? Public relations can be more important to an individual salesperson than to a company. A company has many resources for attracting business. You, the salesperson, have only yourself as a resource. Your *image* is an intangible asset which affects sales as much as your tangible assets (products). The image you should project through PR includes the following elements:

- You care about yourself, your company, your clients, and your community.
- You are an expert in your field.
- You are an accessible professional ready to be of service to clients and non-clients alike.

Public relations involves more than the methods discussed above. The way people see you on a day-to-day basis is also important. For this reason, public relations should be a way of life as well as a strategy for exposure. Professionalism is the best PR.

PUBLICITY

Publicity means getting exposure through the news media. It involves announcements prepared by companies or by the media of newsworthy stories or events. Publicity can also take the form of feature articles in trade magazines. This coverage or "free advertising" often has spectacular results. Publicity often succeeds where advertising fails because of three factors:

1. *Credibility.* When we read an article in the paper or hear a story on the news, we automatically assume they are authentic reports that originated in the media. They gain believability simply because the company selling the product did not sponsor them.

2. *Subtlety.* Your message reaches people in an unobtrusive, indirect way. Publicity can, therefore, reach many prospects who would otherwise resist contact. Prospects "ingest" your message as news rather than as "manipulative rhetoric;" therefore, their defenses are lower.

3. *Dramatization.* Advertising sometimes makes a product or service seem "larger than life." Publicity dramatizes

also, but in a different way. Publicity can convey the message that "we are your neighbors, struggling with you and doing our part to improve life around us." Publicity, especially on a local level, helps create a feeling of community.

Publicity can take many forms. Articles about you or your company prepared by your company or a public relations firm are called *press releases* (see sample on page 180). They are brief, newsworthy stories which highlight the company in a way that is interesting to the public. The difficult step here is getting media representatives to use the story in the newspaper or on the news. To have your press releases published regularly you must have expertise in publicity as well as good connections in the news media. This, of course, does not apply to a good story submitted for the first time. An example of a newsworthy event would be your company discovering a cure for cancer or a new way to manage stress.

Feature articles are excellent sources of publicity. They are written by staff or freelance writers for trade magazines, professional journals, and special business sections of the newspaper. Feature articles cover your business in more depth than press releases. If you're unique in some way as an individual, you may provide an interesting subject for a feature article. For example, let's say that when you were young you were a professional baseball player, and now you're selling space age exercise equipment. You would provide an interesting background in which to set an otherwise boring article. In time, your business would increase due to the publicity.

Photographs are a good vehicle for publicity. Newspapers often print unusual, humorous, and interesting photographs. If you have a photograph which gives some exposure to you or your firm *and* is appealing from a journalistic viewpoint, by all means send it to your local newspaper or trade journal.

Perhaps the most accessible form of publicity is the *Letters to the Editor* section of the paper. If you are abreast of the issues in your town, especially those affecting business, you can express yourself in writing and derive a lot of exposure from it. You'd be surprised how many people actually read the letters to the editor.

Keep in mind that editors mercilessly cut and rewrite publicity articles. To avoid having your article butchered, be sure it's inter-

Gary Beals Marketing Tactics

A Division of California Publicom Inc.

Full Service Advertising, Public Relations and New Business Development Support

8546 Chevy Chase Drive, La Mesa, California 91941-5325

(619) 463-5050   garybeals@home.com   Fax (619) 463-5097

NEWS RELEASE

Friday, June 22, 2001

Contacts:
• Jim Cathcart, Cathcart Institute, Inc. P.O.Box 9075, La Jolla, CA 92038-9075
(858)456-3813   Fax (858)456-7218   www.cathcart.com   info@cathcart.com
• Gary Beals — Gary Beals Marketing Tactics (619) 463-5050 (619) 463-5097 Fax

NOTE TO EDITOR:

A large collection of ideas from Jim Cathcart's 12th book in the field of self-improvement, psychology and business success, "The Acorn Principle"can be provided to you via e-mail. You may use any portions with attribution. Feel free to call Jim directly for an interview. Photographs are available.   Thanks! GB

The Acorn Principle is #2 Best Seller in e-books survey

In the growing category of e-books, San Diego-based professional motivational speaker Jim Cathcart's self-help book is right behind the horror of Steven King, according to a recent survey by Palm Digital Media, a division of Palm, Inc..

The personal growth and business success book by Cathcart, "The Acorn Principle" came in second to Steven King's new book "Riding the Bullet." Books by fiction writer Robert Ludlum and corporate guru Tom Peters trailed the Cathcart book, in third and fourth place, respectively.

"I assume is that right after being scared, people want to learn better ways to understand themselves and reach their goals," Cathcart said with a smile. "'The Acorn Principle' lends itself to the computer-using reader because it is packed with compact checklists and concise guidelines. E-book readers can zero in on ideas they want to reflect on. It's ideal for Palm Pilot-type hand-held devices."

-- more --

esting, timely, factual, accurate, specific, informative, and humble. Any phrases that sound like advertising will be cut.

You should also keep in mind that advertising yields results more quickly than publicity. Advertising is a continual strategy, whereas publicity is usually only occasional unless you use a PR firm to mount an ongoing campaign for you and your company. When you advertise, you have some control over where the ad is placed. Publicity does not entitle you to choose. The editor makes that choice.

An excellent example of serendipity and effective publicity occurred several years ago when the rock star Alice Cooper was in London. The promoters mounted a billboard on a truck and instructed the driver to simply drive around town. As rush hour was approaching, luck would have it that the truck broke down in the middle of a busy intersection. Not only was the traffic tied up for hours, but the media came out to cover "the event." The promoters later acknowledged that they could not have bought better publicity had they tried.

YOUR PROMOTIONAL STRATEGY

As you can see, an effective promotional strategy is multifaceted. The question for you now is, "How do I go about developing a promotional program for myself?" The envelope, please . . . the answer is . . . brainstorming!

First, compile a list of all your publics. You must know whom you're going to reach before you determine how to reach them. Choose the most important prospects and brainstorm all the possible ways of influencing them or impressing them with your positive image. Use the Promotional Strategies Worksheet (7-D) to stimulate your imagination. Let yourself go as you did with the previous brainstorming exercises. Please take the time now to complete this exercise.

Now that you've filled out the Promotional Strategies Worksheet, choose the six techniques that are most effective and affordable at this time. List them in order of priority, starting with those you can do immediately. Then write out your specific goals and the steps you'll take to achieve them. Be sure to follow the rules of goal setting to ensure that each one will come to fruition.

Worksheet 7D
Promotional Strategies Worksheet

DIRECTIONS: Try to list as many creative ways as possible to use the following methods in your promotional program.

ADVERTISING

Radio:

TV:

Trade Magazines:

Newspaper:

Direct Mail:

Ads in Yellow Pages:

Other:

SALES PROMOTIONS

Displays:

Trade Shows/Convention Booths:

Novelties:

Demonstrations:

Other:

PUBLIC RELATIONS

Volunteer Work:

Donations:

Speeches/Seminars:

Holiday Greeting Cards:

Join Clubs/Organizations:

Other:

PUBLICITY

Letters to Editors:

News Releases:

Feature Articles:

Other:

It is rare to find a product or service that "speaks for itself" and doesn't need to be promoted. As professional salespeople, we must recognize that fact, and actively promote ourselves as well as our products or services. Promotional strategies will not only get you in the door, they'll bring the business to you. Together with your prospecting strategies, you'll get prospects *and* business coming and going.

eight

Preparing for the Sales Call

Whereas the sales planning process assesses selling opportunities in your overall market area, the preparation stage assesses selling opportunities for a specific current or potential customer in your territory. Being fully prepared for the sales interview has a number of advantages for both you and the customer. By being prepared, you are better able to react to the demands of the sales transaction. You can talk about those service benefits that relate directly to the needs of the buyer. You can bring the proper materials to the interview so that it progresses smoothly and efficiently. It saves time for the buyer because he is not burdened by an inefficient interview or salesperson. You are able to set realistic call objectives and develop a sales strategy around them. You impress the buyer with your knowledge, preparation, strategy, and confidence. In other words, preparing for sales interviews leads to more, bigger, and better sales. It spells success!

The effective presentation of your product or service to the prospect is a critical point in the marketing process. All the knowledge, skills, attitudes, and efforts you have developed are put into practice at this point. But a sale doesn't just happen . . . it is the *result* of thorough planning and expert execution. An effective sales presentation is the result of thorough planning of all the factors which will influence the customer and motivate him to make a favorable decision.

Now, you must develop a logical, intelligent presentation which will reach the desired goal—the sale. You need to plan *how* to reach the objective, *how* to influence the customer, *how* to make the sale.

Having a sales plan for each customer is nothing more than *selling by objectives*. You should plan before entering a sales situation, rather than reacting to whatever develops in the sales interview. This is not to say that if you preplan you can do without the skills necessary to spot a situation and react quickly. The chances of selling success are much greater if selling instincts are combined with preparation.

You can achieve the highest degree of success in sales simply by planning! The most important planning you can do is the planning of the sales presentation itself, because that's where the final payoffs are realized.

Planning a sales presentation involves nothing more than using common sales sense. You have something to offer your prospects which either provides them a benefit or helps them prevent a loss. Therefore, you plan before the presentation to gear everything you say to achieving either or both of those two objectives.

Obviously, you should know all you can about the prospects upon whom you are calling. Unless you know, you cannot hope to hold their attention to what you have to say. Figuratively, you must "walk in their shoes." You must relate what you say to their needs, their desires, their objectives.

Get to know the real decision maker, along with those who can influence the ultimate decision, within the prospect's company. This vital information should be ascertained as soon as possible. In addition, what is the purchase decision process? Does an individual make the purchase commitment or is it done by a committee? If an individual can make the purchase decision, can she make it only up to a certain dollar amount? Are there any external influences on the decision process, such as attorneys, accountants, consultants, or business advisors?

Once you have an accurate picture of the decision maker and the purchase decision process, you should learn all you can about the prospect, her company, and her industry. You may want to find answers to the following questions.

1. What are the prospect's personal style, idiosyncracies, and temperament?
2. What are her hobbies, sports, and pastimes?
3. How about his family and their interests?
4. Does she buy on opinion or fact; friendship or reciprocity?
5. What is his present product usage?
6. What is my present or potential competition for this account?
7. What are her specific needs for my service?
8. Why should he purchase from me rather than one of my competitors?
9. What is her volume of business?
10. What type and quality of merchandise does he carry?
11. How does she market her merchandise?
12. What is his credit rating?
13. Are there any trends within her industry that might affect the purchase decision now or in the future?

The more questions you can answer, the better prepared you will be for your sales interview and the more likely to achieve a successful outcome.

Choosing Activities

Your primary activity in preparing for a sales call will be research. You'll want to know who to contact, their possible needs, their financial status, when they may want to buy, and who your competitors are. If you're well organized, this task will be far easier. Be sure to take advantage of your company as a source of information. Your prospect may be a former or present client of your company. In this case, a file will already exist which can provide all the information you need.

It is helpful to have a checklist or worksheet to use as a guide when doing research. After completing the worksheet you will know exactly where you stand with the prospect. Our Sales Planning Guide covers the information you need for planning and preparation. We have included a sample worksheet to show you how informative they can be. Adapt the form to your needs and use one for each prospect you research.

Information Needed before a Sales Call

The more information you have about a prospect, the better your chances of making a sale. The Sales Planning Guide (Form 8-A) provides your information on the prospect's background. Any time you do not have most (if not all) of the information listed on this guide, you are doing "cold call" selling, even though you may have made an appointment for a presentation. In this case, however, it is not the call that is cold; it is you.

By contrast, knowing as much as you possibly can know about your prospects, their needs and wants, and the services you can provide will help you get a favorable commitment.

Some basic areas covered in the Sales Planning Guide need to be explored as part of your pre-call homework. These are covered step by step in the following sections.

Who is the decision maker?   When you make your sales call you don't want to waste your time. It is imperative that you meet with someone who is in a decision-making position. This person must also be knowledgeable enough to know what you are talking about. If you discover that this person does not have the authority to buy or to make decisions, you must diplomatically find out how the system works or whom you must see. Some company structures require the completion of a long chain of events before a decision can be made. If this is the case, ask your prospect, "Would you give me an idea of your company's decision-making process for a purchase such as this?" If that process involves more than one person seeing your presentation, try to arrange to show everyone at once. In some cases, however, it will be necessary for you to show several people your product at different times.

What is your prospect's current situation?   In order to get a feel for the climate of your prospect's business, you need to ask some general questions. You might start off by suggesting, "Tell me a little bit about your business." This is a safe, nonthreatening opener which can lead the way to more in-depth probing such as "What's happening with sales?" or "Are you encountering any

Form 8-A
Sales Planning Guide

Company _____ _____ Type of Business_____

Location_____ Phone_____Date_____

Key Contact_____ Title_____

Who is the decision maker?_____

Current Situation?

Goals and Objectives?

Potential Problem(s)/Need(s)

What objectives should I seek to accomplish with this account?

Next call:

Overall:

If the key contact is not the decision maker, how can he/she influence the objective(s) I am trying to achieve?

What questions can I ask to uncover, clarify, or amplify prospect problems, needs, and/or goals?

What decision-making criteria are important to this prospect?

Form 8-A continued

Possible benefits and proof materials prospect is seeking	Features that provide those benefits	(Letters, testimonials) to be used if necessary

How can I be of more benefit to this prospect than anyone else who has called on him/her?

Possible prospect objections   Potential answers

Based on my objective(s), what specific commitment will I ask this prospect to make?

Why should the prospect want to make this commitment?

By what criteria will the prospect judge whether or not my product/service/company was a satisfactory solution to his problem/need?

What methods, procedures, or forms can I use to measure whether or not the actual results did in fact meet the above criteria?

special problems with your present product or service?" You'll need to adapt these questions to your industry, however. You can see that some delicate probing can identify needs that might otherwise have remained hidden.

What are your prospects' goals? Aside from making money, what are they trying to accomplish in business? Forget about your product or service for a moment and get a grasp of the overall picture. Once you understand a company's primary purpose in the marketplace, you'll be able to relate to it in a more relevant way. This will also show them that you are interested in their business and well-being in addition to making sales.

Does your prospect have potential problems and needs? Once you determine your prospect's current situation and goals and objectives, you can readily determine if a "need gap" exists. A need gap exists when the prospect's current situation is not living up to or accomplishing his desired situation (objectives or end results). The greater the need gap, the greater and more immediate the need for the prospect to change what he's currently doing or purchasing. The greater the need gap, the greater the probability for you to make a sale.

You might also think about what the consequences could be if they don't use your product or service. Having that insight, you can develop some very strong and well thought out selling points to use in your presentation.

What Are Your Call Objectives?

Every time you see a client, you should have a reason for making that call. Dropping by to say hello is nice, but may be a waste of time. If you want to be sociable, you can use the phone. If you haven't sold the prospect yet, your reason for stopping by should be one of the action steps that will move you closer to making the sale. For example, you might stop by to show the prospect the latest in your product line or a new service you have to offer. Each time you see your prospect you should try to learn more about his or her needs. Ideally, each call will produce tangible evidence that you are making progress with the prospect; otherwise, you're just going through the motions.

Probing Questions to Uncover Needs

Although it is not generally advisable to have specifically worded questions that you will ask in a particular sequence, it is advisable to have a questioning strategy. This simply means that you should have a general idea of what you would like to ask in order to get the particular information you require. A questioning plan gives you a starting point but also allows you the flexibility to explore additional fruitful areas as they arise in the conversation. When you leave your planned questions to explore these other beneficial areas, you can use directive questions to bring you back on track. Remember that you need only a hazy idea of the type of information you desire as well as the types of questions you need to ask to get that information. You do not need specifically worded questions prior to your interview.

What are the decision making criteria?   Part of your research should uncover the reason(s) why your prospect might be interested in your product or service. This is almost independent of need. You've already established or suspect a strong need, but why is that need present?

Once you have this information, you can look for the criteria used by each person you speak to in the company. In general you know that an executive will be interested in the long-term goals of the company or in increasing overall sales and profits. A middle manager will base his opinion on the cost effectiveness of your product while the first-line supervisors will be concerned with installation and operation.

When you contact each of these individuals, be aware of their different perspectives and gear your presentation to the criteria upon which their decision will be based. Everyone wants to know if the purchase will benefit them. If you can show everyone along the line that they, too, will benefit, then you'll be a strong contender in the race for their business.

Decision-making criteria can also relate to "constraints" on the final decision, such as budget limits, quantity and size requirements, delivery, or other factors. It is crucial to determine these decision-making requirements as early as possible in the sales interview to ensure that *you* can meet them. For instance, if delivery must be made within 5 days and the earliest you can possibly deliver is in 14 days, you have a problem. You can either attempt to "negotiate" this constraint to a mutually acceptable delivery time frame (e.g., 10 days), or you may have to walk away from the sale. As you can see, decision-making criteria are crucial prospect "qualifiers" that should tell you whether or not it is worth your time to pursue this specific account.

How will you have to prove yourself? After you've presented your ideas and created some interest, many prospects will want you to prove your claims. They may ask you for a demonstration or an opportunity to try out the product in their business. An easier and less time-consuming way to prove your product or service is to offer testimonials from people the prospects know and trust. Being able to say, "Your friend Ajax, Inc. down the street bought one last year and is very happy with it. Susan St. James in accounting told me you should call her if you want to hear more about it." This can be very convincing to a prospect.

If you can find out in advance what means will be necessary to prove yourself, you can spend time preparing to make your proof effective and appropriate to your prospect's needs.

What is your competitive edge? Is there something about you that is unique? Something which gives you the advantage over other companies and salespeople? If so, use it to your advantage. Often a minor detail will tip the balance in your direction. Many sales have been made based on the statement, "In addition to the product, you also get me. I come with the package. I'll be here when you need me to make sure that everything runs smoothly and that you realize the full benefits of the product." That kind of enthusiasm and sincerity makes salespeople winners!

During your presentation, highlight your unique selling factors. This is an excellent time to admit a limitation in your product. The customer will find out about it anyway, so you might as well score some points by being the one to enlighten him or her. When pointing out a weak point, contrast it with a strong point For example, if you're selling dictation machines and say, "Yet, it's true that my machine will not take a standard cassette. The microcassettes are, however, much easier to store and take up less room in your briefcase. They're actually easier to carry with you." That's honest selling which shows you are different from the rest.

What objections are you likely to encounter?   When you're rehearsing your presentation, either with someone or in your mind, try imagining what the prospect's reactions will be. What questions will be asked? What resistance will you encounter from skeptical people? If you know the potential objections and questions, then you have time to prepare yourself. You can study your product and company until you have every possible question answered. By doing so, you will be able to quell your prospect's fears with smooth, confident, and truthful answers. You will find this to be time well spent because there's nothing worse than stammering and struggling to answer a prospect's question. When you do, your credibility often takes a nose dive.

What commitment will you ask?   It is essential, at the end of a sales call, to know what action will follow. The only way to know this is to confirm it with the prospect in the form of a verbal agreement. There are all kinds of things you might ask for: more information, a referral, permission to give a demonstration, or, best of all, for the order itself!

Regardless of the commitment you seek, before you make the call you should have in mind a specific end result for the meeting. This is the most important part of your call objective.

How will you know the success criteria?   Many products, such as business computers, serve different functions for different clients. If your product or service falls into this category how will *you* know if it is benefiting the client or not? You know some of the improvements he or she wants to make, but you can't know them all. So ask your client, "What are the criteria that you will use to judge the effectiveness of this product?" Your client will tell you what they are looking for and when they hope to see results. You should make a note of this and follow up at the appropriate time. Even if the follow-up is months later, you must carry through in order to keep your professional reputation intact and your client happy.

There's an old adage—"If you fail to plan then you are planning to fail." In sales, this couldn't be more true. Your research and preparation will educate you so that you *will* be of service to your client. If you don't prepare yourself, you might as well be calling everyone cold without even knowing their names. It's not a very attractive alternative. Preparation and planning are like studying a map: You'll know which road to take with your prospect to get where you *both* want to go.

nine

The Last Chapter— Where Do You Go from Here?

We have come a long way together since Chapter 1. In Chapters 2, 3, and 4, we covered the key self-management skills of professional image, goal setting, and time management. The all-important sales planning skills were covered in the following four chapters. Territory management and target marketing were covered in Chapter 5; prospecting and promotional strategies were discussed in Chapters 6 and 7; and call preparation was examined in Chapter 8. Now we have arrived at the last chapter. Where do you go from here?

Where you go depends totally on you. You have just been exposed to a new experience and have seen a new way to view, analyze, and conduct the professional sales process.

You can respond to this new experience in one of five ways:

1. You can integrate the new experience with your past experiences because the new experience is perceived as pleasant and compatible.

2. You might totally reject this new experience because it is perceived as too threatening.

3. You can isolate the new experience from what you are accustomed to and thereby treat it as an exception to the rule. This allows you to continue acting and thinking as you have done customarily.

4. You might distort this new experience to make it "fit" your past experiences.

5. Finally, you can perceive the experience as a new reality and change your old ways of thinking and acting to conform to your newly expanded or newly perceived reality.

The most productive of these five reactions is the last one. By reacting in accordance with this response, you undergo a positive behavioral change. Don't just accept everything that you have read, of course. Instead, you take what makes sense to you and weave it into your current "reality." Nothing that you have seen in this book is cast in concrete. Which segments you choose to use and how you use them will ultimately determine your sales effectiveness—now and in the future.

We would be extremely pleased if, after reading this book, you went out and started practicing the "business of selling" philosophy. It won't be easy, though. It will take practice, some mistakes, and more practice to lead eventually to your successful implementation of these strategies.

Can you remember when you first learned to drive a car? Before you ever learned, you were what we call an "unconscious incompetent." That is, you didn't know how to drive. When you first went out with one of your parents, a friend, or an instructor to learn how to actually drive the car, you became a "conscious incompetent." You still couldn't drive the car, but because of your new awareness of the automobile and its parts, you were consciously aware of why you couldn't drive it. From this step, you at least had the awareness of what you had to learn and do to acquire the competency to drive.

With some additional practice and guidance, you were able to become competent in driving the car. However, you had to be consciously aware of what you were doing with all the mechanical aspects of the car as well as with your body. You had to be consciously aware to turn on your blinker signals well before you executed a turn. You had to remember to monitor the traffic behind you in your rearview mirror. You kept both hands on the wheel and monitored your car's position relative to the centerline road divider. You were consciously aware of all these things as you drove. We call this phase of learning "conscious competence."

Think of the last time you drove a car. Were you consciously aware of all the things we've just discussed? Of course not! Most of us, after having driven for a while, progress to a level of "unconscious competence." This is the level where we can do something well without even thinking about it. It comes naturally.

The foregoing example holds true for your use of the sales strategies discussed in this book. You must go through the four levels of competence in order to get to the highest level—the unconscious competence level. Achieving that level means you can manage yourself and plan your sales efforts naturally and successfully. If you can get to that level, you should see a marked increase in your sales productivity. However, you must pay a price to get to the level of unconscious competence: practice, practice, practice.

When you were learning to drive the car, you acquired your competency through practice. The same holds true for the "business of selling" skills. This may require a change of behavior from your present method of selling. If this is the case, expect to see a *decrease* in your sales productivity initially. This is a common occurrence in behavioral change. However, after *persistence* and *practice*—and as you approach the unconscious competency level—your sales productivity will increase beyond its previous level and form a new and higher plateau. You'll be able to make more sales with even less effort!

Make An Action Plan

So you've decided to accept the challenge! The payoffs are certainly well worth your efforts. Now you must meet the challenge. With so much to learn about self-management, sales planning, sales communications, and conversational selling skills, you are probably confused about where to start. How do you create an effective action plan that will meet your needs?

Our advice is to first clarify your objectives and assess your current situation. Then ask yourself, how well do I manage my time? Probe? Set goals? Listen? Read body language? Give and receive feedback? Target markets? Manage my present accounts? Prospect? Prepare for sales calls?

As you determine your current situation in each of these domains and compare it with your new objectives, identify problem areas that need work. There may be a number of areas, but take care to set priorities on problem areas according to how much attention they need. First work on the areas that need the most help. As you become more competent, go on to the lower-priority problem areas. Develop an action plan specifically to improve those areas that will help you in your quest to become a strategic, professional salesperson. Specifically define ways to accomplish your action plan. Set up an implementation schedule and establish commitment to follow it through according to scheduled completion times. Set goals and establish your criteria for success; determine how and when to measure your performance in improving your strategic selling skills. Constantly monitor your results and take corrective action where and when necessary. Priorities, focus, intensity, goals, strategies, deadlines, and measurements will become your keys to success.

Your new action plan might include further professional help in the form of seminars, books, or tapes. Keep informed of other learning devices that will help you improve any or all of the skills discussed in this book. Your plan may also include a more detailed review of relevant portions of this book when appropriate.

Correctly used, the "business of selling" skills will allow you to interact with your prospects and solve their problems in an open, honest atmosphere of trust and helpfulness. Your prospects and clients will gain relevant solutions to their needs and problems. You will deservedly feel an increased pride in your new successful selling style—the "business of selling" style.

You needn't wait; you can start to apply these sales skills immediately. The path has been mapped. Where do you go from here? Only *you* know which path you'll take. Good luck!

Printed in the United States
3484

9 780962 516139